MW00593608

This book belongs to

_____

Walk with Me, Jesus

DAILY WORDS OF HOPE AND ENCOURAGEMENT

Marie Chapian

BroadStreet
PUBLISHING

BroadStreet Publishing® Group, LLC.
Savage, Minnesota, USA.
Broadstreetpublishing.com

Walk with Me, Jesus: Daily Words of Hope and Encouragement
© 2015 Marie Chapian
978-1-4245-5048-7 (hardcover)
978-1-4245-6068-4 (faux leather)
978-1-4245-5049-4 (e-book)

Design by Chris Garborg | garborgdesign.com
Edited by Michelle Winger | literallyprecise.com

Printed in China.
20 21 22 23 24 25 26   7 6 5 4 3 2 1

Guide me in your truth and teach me,

for you are God my Savior,

and my hope is in you all day long.

PSALM 25:5 NIV

Introduction

THESE DAILY MEDITATIONS FROM THE HEART OF GOD ARE AIMED DIRECTLY AT YOUR HEART. GOD SPEAKS OPENLY AND SIMPLY BECAUSE HE LOVES YOU. HE WANTS YOU TO WALK IN THE PROMISE OF HIS BLESSING AND ABIDING FRIENDSHIP ALL YEAR LONG.

EVERY TIME WE PRAY, "WALK WITH ME, JESUS," HE WILL ALWAYS ANSWER: "COME."

MAY YOUR LIFE BE ENRICHED AND YOUR FAITH DEEPENED WHEN YOU OPEN THIS BOOK EVERY DAY TO HEAR FROM HIM.

WITH SO MUCH LOVE,

Marie Chapian

JANUARY

"Seek first the kingdom of God and
His righteousness, and all these things
shall be added to you."

MATTHEW 6:33 NKJV

January 1

Today, don't just live–
live your fullest.
Rise up and take your divine calling
in Me to a higher level
at the beginning of this new year.
The beauty of your presence isn't skin-deep;
it's spirit-deep.
Your presence brings the aroma of heaven with you.
You're going to spread your wings
and soar high like eagles this year.
You're going to run and not get tired.
You're going to walk and not fall behind.
Today, look into the mirror of your soul
and see Me!
Rise up in the fullness
of your life and enjoy running
and walking in a world blessed
by your spirit-blessed presence.

Those who wait for the Lord will gain new strength;
they will mount up with wings like eagles,
they will run and not get tired,
they will walk and not become weary.

ISAIAH 40:31 NASB

January 2

Acknowledge the small things
in your life today.
Learn from the things you drop
and pick up, and drop again.
Learn from listening.
Learn from your sweet acts
of patience and tolerance.
Be happier because of this day.
There's much to learn
from the small things
you ordinarily take for granted.
A single blade of grass
in the wind can teach you much.
Honor this day and be thankful.
Your thankful heart is the heart of eternity.

Oh, that men would give thanks to the LORD for His goodness,
and for His wonderful works to the children of men!

PSALM 107:8 NKJV

January 3

I care about your whole self.
There isn't one aspect of your life
that I'm not concerned about.
Emotions can often hurt
the deepest, even more
than physical disruptions.
I can heal the most hidden hurts
of your heart, so I ask you
to release everything to Me today.
I'm here to renew and refresh you
in your body and your soul.
I'm here to show you a new way
of loving and believing in yourself,
so you'll stand strong and not waver
from the work that's set before you.

**He heals the brokenhearted
and bandages their wounds.**

PSALM 147:3 NCV

January 4

There's no shame anywhere around
when you're locked in tight with Me,
because I'm the one who wipes out
all of your soul blunders and transgressions
for My own sake.
I absolutely will not remember
your sins, so this means
you're positively free
to be all you can be
as a vibrant, cleaned up,
pure and wholesome child of God.
You're good now,
so drop the past and anything that'll keep you
from the good life I planned for you
from the beginning.
Trust Me, dear one.
You have a beautiful future.

I will forgive their wickedness,
and I will never again remember their sins.

HEBREWS 8:12 NLT

January 5

Don't be anxious about anything today.
Tell Me what you need
with a thankful heart,
knowing I'm answering you.
I want you to experience inner peace
that far surpasses human understanding
because it's this peace that stands guard
over your heart and your mind.
Fix your mind on the things
that are true, noble, just, pure, lovely,
reputable, and praiseworthy.
Think about what's beautiful, not ugly;
things that are good, not evil.
Stop robbing yourself by pondering
the wrong things,
and focus on enriching your life
with goodness.

Keep your thoughts continually fixed on all that is authentic and real,
honorable and admirable, beautiful and respectful, pure and holy,
merciful and kind. And fasten your thoughts on every glorious work
of God, praising him always.

PHILIPPIANS 4:8 TPT

January 6

Today is a day to turn to your friends
for strength and support.
I've said that if two of you agree on earth
about anything that you ask for,
it'll be done for you by My Father in heaven.
There's great strength, love, and comfort
to be had with your friends.
Don't be shy about asking for help when you need it.
When you're together with friends in My name,
I'm there in your midst.
I love unity and the fervent pursuit
to see My will done.
You need one another.
As you're strengthened, helped, and encouraged
by others, you're doing the same for them.
This is a gift you give and receive, and it's My will.

"If two of you agree on earth about anything that they may ask, it shall
be done for them by My Father who is in heaven. For where two or
three have gathered together in My name, I am there in their midst."

Matthew 18:19–20 NASB

January 7

Creation and goodness are synonymous
with Me, so today focus on that which is good.
It's altogether too easy for you to fill your mind
with unpleasant stuff.
When you focus on My good benefits
and all the goodness I've surrounded you with,
you'll attract more goodness to yourself,
which in turn will become an impenetrable wall
against negativity and soul-harm.
Your Father in heaven who loves you
didn't create anything in the earth realm
that's not good. Every good
and perfect gift comes from God,
and you're the crowning glory
of everything created.
See and recognize
the goodness around you and in you.
Today, treat yourself as My crowning glory.

Every gift God freely gives us is good and perfect, streaming down
from the Father of lights, who shines from the heavens with
no hidden shadow or darkness and is never subject to change.

JAMES 1:17 TPT

January 8

I want to have the opportunity
to operate in your life
through the words you speak today.
Be extra-aware of the words you speak today
because that tongue of yours is a powerful tool.
It possesses the power of death and life,
so think about what you say.
Consider your words a creative force that can birth
joy and hope, as well as misery.
The things you talk about during the day
can produce life and happiness,
or they can kill and wreck things.
Choose your words,
dear one, choose them carefully,
and let Me speak through you.

Death and life are in the power of the tongue,
and those who love it will eat its fruits.

Proverbs 18:21 NRSV

January 9

Realize you have unlimited resources
in you.
The more you acknowledge
and recognize the favor
I give you in your life,
the more you'll be able
to believe what I can do
in the lives of others through you.
Use what you have from Me
to help others and build them up.

"You are the salt of the earth, but if salt has lost its taste, how shall its saltiness be restored? It is no longer good for anything except to be thrown out and trampled under people's feet. You are the light of the world. A city set on a hill cannot be hidden. Nor do people light a lamp and put it under a basket, but on a stand, and it gives light to all in the house. In the same way, let your light shine before others, so that they may see your good works and give glory to your Father who is in heaven."

MATTHEW 5:13-16 ESV

January 10

My Holy Spirit isn't restricted
by dreams or desires that you think
are too big to fulfill.
Pay attention
to the enormity of your potential.
My Holy Spirit is working for you,
so knock
and keep on knocking.
Persevere!
No dream of yours is too big.

"Ask, and it will be given to you; seek, and you will find;
knock, and it will be opened to you."

MATTHEW 7:7 NASB

January 11

I love to answer your prayers.
Your answered prayers
bring glory to Me.
I've made you a model
of answered prayer.
From now on be allergic to anything
that tries to diminish My power
to answer prayer.
Stand fast.
Be strong and resolute,
and you'll know for certain
that I can never fail you.
Live who you are today and serve Me
even if it's without receiving credit.
I'll reward you. I see everything.

"Whatever things you ask in prayer, believing, you will receive."

MATTHEW 21:22 NKJV

January 12

Don't be afraid of problems.
Don't shrink from them.
Don't you know you were created for problems?
No one on earth can handle problems
like you because you're empowered within
to rise above the snares and barbs
of the world to prevail
in all circumstances.
My Spirit in you is greater
than any problem you'll ever face.
It's by My Spirit that you rise up
and take the authority
I've given you to overcome and come out on top.
Today, be brave.
Be strong.
Be fabulous for Me.

You belong to God, my dear children. You have already won a victory
over those people, because the Spirit who lives in you is greater than
the spirit who lives in the world.

1 John 4:4 nlt

January 13

I'm unchanging love.
I'm your love and we're beautiful together.
See Me for who I am today,
and you'll see yourself
for who you are. There's no way
to truly know yourself without looking
into the mirror of heaven,
and seeing your reflection there.
I've written you on the palms of My hands,
and your name
is on the dotted line in My Book of Life,
so it's time to become familiar
with the beautiful aspects
and qualities of yourself
that reflect My aspects and qualities.
I want you to respect
who you are as My child today
because when you do,
you'll walk in wisdom and integrity
and avoid much heartache.

Can't you see? I have carved your name on the palms of my hands!

ISAIAH 49:16 TPT

January 14

Healing and victory are yours.
In the mind of the Father
you're a hero.
You're a conqueror.
Whoever is born of God overcomes the world
and its many troubles.
My triumph on the cross is your triumph.
My victory over death is your victory.
All that I did when
I was on the earth was for you,
just for you, so you could live
an abundant life now,
dynamic, whole, and undefeated.
Take what's yours today and live!

He was pierced for our transgressions,
he was crushed for our iniquities;
the punishment that brought us peace was on him,
and by his wounds we are healed.

ISAIAH 53:5 NIV

January 15

I'm a God of abundance, and I've promised
to bless you in all things.
When you talk on about your lack of strength
or ability, you're giving credit
to your adversary for blinding you to the truth
of the abundance you possess.
Yes, things can be discouraging. I understand,
but let Me hold you up.
Throw your doubts and worries into the pit
with your adversary, the devil.
I'll never leave you to figure things out
on your own without direction
and intervention; never.
You always have My love
caressing and watching over you
even when it feels like
you're a million miles away from Me.
It's impossible for Me to break a promise.
Believe today, and look inside at
what wonderful faith burns in you.

The tested genuineness of your faith—more precious than gold that
perishes though it is tested by fire—may be found to result in praise and
glory and honor at the revelation of Jesus Christ.

1 PETER 1:7 ESV

January 16

Who are you afraid of?
You're redeemed from every earthly curse.
Shake off your heavy chains today.
You aren't who you used to be.
The old you is gone, out of the picture.
Forget about it.
Proclaim today that I'm your strength
and your wisdom. Proclaim that I'm
your complete and perfect new life.
In Me you aren't the person you once were.
I've given you a new heart with a new capacity
for deeper love
and greater understanding.
Use what I've given you today.

I will give you a new heart,
and I will put a new spirit in you.
I will take out your stony, stubborn heart
and give you a tender, responsive heart.

EZEKIEL 36:26 NLT

January 17

Believe My Word
and believe what I have given you today
to be strong in the world.
Get up, take the authority I have given you
and proclaim your healing.
Proclaim what is yours as My child.
Every time you talk about your troubles
you weaken your faith.
Talk about what I've overcome for you.
Talk about the blessings
I've blessed you with and the everlasting love
that has forgiven you of every sin.
Talk about how strong you are in Me
and show the world who you are.

I have been crucified with Christ; it is no longer I who live,
but Christ lives in me; and the life which I now live in the flesh
I live by faith in the Son of God, who loved me
and gave Himself for me.

GALATIANS 2:20 NKJV

January 18

Faith is a wonderful gift, dear one,
and when you beg Me for faith
you tend to focus on
what you think you don't have.
I say exercise what you do have!
Yes, you have faith, and when you
focus on what you think
you don't have, you increase doubt
about yourself and about Me.
Don't you see?
You're praying for what I've already given you!
When I tell you that I know My thoughts
toward you, it means My thoughts
are on you continually.
I know what I'm thinking about at all times!
I know Myself and I know My mind.
You live in My mind.
Allow Me to live in your mind.

"For I know the plans I have for you," says the LORD.
"They are plans for good and not for disaster,
to give you a future and a hope."

JEREMIAH 29:11 NLT

January 19

I'm giving you new insight into things,
but you must remain positive and confident
that the details of your life are working together
for good, and I know what I'm doing.
Things are going to become clearer to you
as you step forward in faith
assured that I'm in control.
Nothing can defeat you when heaven
lives in you.
Think about this.
You can go through anything
and endure anything because inside you
lives the majestic and glorious power
and presence of heaven.
I am heaven. I am all-in-all,
so bolster yourself up
with a new surge of confidence now.

Put on the new self who is being renewed to a true knowledge
according to the image of the One who created him.

COLOSSIANS 3:10 NASB

January 20

Fill your words with grace today.
Be gentle, be kind,
for there's great reward in kindness,
demonstrating the generosity of God.
When you show acts of kindness,
no matter how small,
you're acting in agreement
with My desires to release blessings
into the world.
You're called to live
in the blessing you're blessed with,
so show yourself thoughtful.
Be ever on the lookout to do good
and bring acts and words of kindness
wherever you go.

We prove ourselves by our purity, our understanding, our patience,
our kindness, by the Holy Spirit within us, and by our sincere love.

2 CORINTHIANS 6:6 NLT

January 21

I'm increasing your creativity.
Write down your ideas and your thoughts.
Allow Me to speak to you and show you
new ways of handling problems
and concerns that are too big for you alone.
As you pray and ask for direction and guidance,
I'll answer you with revelation and understanding
into My Word and into your life situation.
Expect divinely inspired ideas.
Pay attention to them and meditate
on all that I give you
and you'll see much fruit as a result.

Their wisdom will guide you wherever you go
and keep you from bringing harm to yourself.
Their instruction will whisper to you at every sunrise
and direct you through a brand-new day.
For truth is a bright beam of light shining into every area of your life,
instructing and correcting you to discover the ways to godly living.

PROVERBS 6:22-23 TPT

January 22

It's time to act on
that which you've been putting off.
The time has come to do something
you haven't wanted to do.
New spiritual gifts and blessings
are waiting for you
as you take the necessary steps
to accomplish the things
you've been ignoring
and putting off for later.
It's your day of break-through,
so be brave and plunge ahead
to get the task done.
Don't be afraid; I'm with you!

Whatever you do, do it heartily, as to the Lord and not to men,
knowing that from the Lord you will receive the reward of the
inheritance; for you serve the Lord Christ.

Colossians 3:23-24 NKJV

January 23

What things in your life
are weighing you down today?
Are your own thoughts about yourself
obstructing My thoughts toward you?
Examine your doubts and your fears
to see if they line up with My purposes
and plans for your life as I've made clear
in My Word.
I've made you necessary
in the world and I am guiding you
by My hand perfectly.
What you consider a devastating detour
is to Me a simple hiccough along the way.
Never allow your thoughts
to stray into the dark corners of self-doubt.
Be confident today in your calling
and in My complete, undying love for you.

He has rescued us completely from the tyrannical rule of darkness and
has translated us into the kingdom realm of his beloved Son.

COLOSSIANS 1:13 TPT

January 24

There always seems
to be too much to do, dear one.
More people and more responsibilities
are asking for your time.
You can't do it all on your own,
so lean on Me rather than
your own strength.
This is the moment
to lean on others to help you.
I've not called you to stressful, endless labor.
You're not an island.
Don't be ashamed to reach out for help.
I'll give you others to share the load,
and doing so you'll see a multiplication
of blessing on all you accomplish.
You'll create more happiness and lasting fruit
when you include others.

"What you are doing is not good. You will surely wear yourself out,
both you and these people with you. For the task is too heavy for you;
you cannot do it alone."

EXODUS 18:17-18 NRSV

January 25

I find no fault in you, dear one,
for your sins have been forgiven.
I don't define your future by your past.
Your future is defined by My will
and My love for you,
not by what's taken place in the past.
Shame and doubt belong at the foot
of the cross because I want
sunshine and light to shower upon you.
Bundle up every sin,
mistake, and wrong choice and chuck them
in the garbage bin of forgiven dead stuff.
I never visit there and neither should you.
What's finished is finished;
jump into new life today with joy.

"I, yes I, am the One and Only, who completely erases your sins,
never to be seen again. I will not remember them again.
Freely I do this because of who I am!"

ISAIAH 43:25 TPT

January 26

Be happy today
because I want you to know
I'm taking care of you.
You become strong
when you listen to Me
and you follow My ways,
like a tree planted by a thriving river.
The tree produces fruit and its leaves don't die.
Obey Me and be happy. Show Me
that you're loyal and that you trust Me.
You're happiest when you trust Me,
not just sometimes, but at all times,
morning and night.
I'm your Lord
and I'm your best friend.

Happy are those who don't listen to the wicked, who don't go where sinners go, who don't do what evil people do. They love the LORD's teachings, and they think about those teachings day and night. They are strong, like a tree planted by a river. The tree produces fruit in season, and its leaves don't die. Everything they do will succeed.

PSALM 1:1-3 NCV

January 27

I'm here to give you courage.
When you pray I'm right here
listening. You can lie down
and go to sleep and be at peace
because I'm renewing and strengthening you
in slumber.
Thousands of problems amass
around you, but don't be afraid.
I'll rescue you from the wolves
in the night and the troubles that whizz through the air
in the daytime, as well.
I'll always answer when you pray.
Dear child, you can trust Me
to do what's right and in alignment
with My purposes and your calling.

**You will not fear the terror of night,
nor the arrow that flies by day.**

PSALM 91:5 NIV

January 28

Tell Me what you need every morning
knowing I'll answer every need.
Because of your sweet love for Me,
it's a joy to answer you.
I love to show you the right thing to do.
and how I want you to live
because you listen.
You bring Me much pleasure,
My love.
Ask and keep on asking.

Let me hear Your lovingkindness in the morning;
For I trust in You; teach me the way in which I should walk;
For to You I lift up my soul.

PSALM 143:8 NASB

January 29

Trust Me for protection.
Know that I save and rescue you.
Don't condemn yourself
thinking you've done something wrong
to keep Me from solving ongoing problems
and answering long-standing prayers.
Your enemy is My enemy.
I do what's right.
I know how you feel as you watch and wait,
and I'm beside you, with you, and in you.
I observe how you
handle every troublesome situation
in your life, and it's your faith I applaud!
It's the immeasurable power
of faith that stirs the halls of heaven and My heart.
I tell you, your faith will accomplish great things!
Stay strong!

Lord, you are a paradise of protection to me.
You lift me high above the fray.
None of my foes can touch me when I'm held
firmly in your wrap-around presence!

Psalm 61:3 tpt

January 30

Let My words to you today
be like smooth, delicious honey.
My words are like summer fruit, their juice
dripping down into your heart where they
create more sweet fruit.
My words are meant
to give you new strength and to make you wise.
They're meant to make you happy.
My words are pure like the sun,
and they'll light your way today and every day.
My judgments are true and completely right.
There are no shadowy spots
in My communication with you.
My words are worth more than the purest gold.
Respect My Word and let the honey of My love
delight you and fill you with courage and renewed purpose.
Think about Me. Speak to Me.
Love Me. I'm your rock:
the sweet and powerful author of all there is,
and I'm the lover of your soul.

The orders of the LORD are right: they make people happy. The
commands of the LORD are pure; they light up the way. Respect for the
LORD is good; it will last forever. The judgments of the LORD are true;
they are completely right. They are worth more than gold, even the
purest gold. They are sweeter than honey, even the finest honey.

PSALM 19:8-10 NCV

January 31

If you feel you've let Me down,
look at each new day
as a transformed beginning,
fresh and beautiful
and filled with hope.
Your capacity for love
is inexhaustible by My Spirit
and in no way limited.
If you ever feel you've let Me down,
know that you can't scare Me off easily,
for I know your future and the vastness
of your potential.
Together
you and I will walk the high places
of the world.

Therefore my heart is glad and my tongue rejoices;
my body also will rest secure.

PSALM 16:9 NIV

FEBRUARY

Your word is a lamp to my feet

And a light to my path.

PSALM 119:105 NKJV

February 1

When I call you to obey My voice,
it gives Me pleasure to see your response.
I love your tender heart
and your zeal to serve others
and the hurting world.
I love how you open your heart to Me
each day, and invite Me into your life.
Your mind is occupied
with Me and I want you to know
that you bring
your heavenly Father much joy
when you release My love
through your tender heart.

Walk in a manner worthy of the Lord, fully pleasing to him: bearing
fruit in every good work and increasing in the knowledge of God.

COLOSSIANS 1:10 ESV

February 2

I see what you can't see.
I know what you don't know.
Our hearts are one heart and you can trust Me
to accomplish My will concerning you.
I gave you the sacred gift
of choice in all things,
so today choose to be strong.
I've directed the love of all heaven
toward you so you'll prevail
with honor in your situation.
Some hearts you encounter are dark
and won't budge from the bleak ruts
of deception, but don't be dismayed.
Maintain your integrity.
Stay bold, daring, and determined.
I have a harvest that's ripe
and waiting for you.

"I am in them and you are in me.
May they experience such perfect unity that the world
will know that you sent me and that you love them
as much as you love me."

JOHN 17:23 NLT

February 3

Sometimes the world is a cruel magnet
pulling you this way and that,
but if you'll listen
to Me and obey My voice,
you'll have nothing to fear.
I'll give you strength to stand strong
for goodness and truth.
I gave you a world to love
and to bring your happy heart to,
but it's not My desire to see
the world eat up your joy
with its ravenous tongue and temptations.
You're beautiful to Me, and I'm calling you
to draw closer to Me today where you're safe,
honored with grace, and completely loved.

The Lord has appeared of old to me, saying:
"Yes, I have loved you with an everlasting love;
Therefore with lovingkindness I have drawn you."

JEREMIAH 31:3 NKJV

February 4

When the world around you
seems uncertain and you feel
helpless, return to the stability
of your foundation.
When you feel vulnerable and fearful,
hurl yourself into the arms of truth.
Establish your inner man by forming
dynamic thought patterns
solidly fixed on the truth of My Word.
Hold onto My security guarantee
with perfect hope and trust.
Never allow yourself to slip
into the pot holes of worry and confusion.
When gloom floods the horizon
of your mind, turn your thoughts
to My thoughts and My plans.
You're safe in Me, and
I have big plans for you.

We know that for those who love God
all things work together for good, for those
who are called according to his purpose.

ROMANS 8:28 ESV

February 5

Think for a moment about the children of God
in the past who loved Me and held on through
what seemed hopeless situations.
Think of Moses traveling the hot, dry desert
for forty long years with no likelihood of change.
Think of Joseph, an innocent man,
hurled in a dark, dank prison
for twelve years with no hope of release.
Think of Daniel tossed into a den
with hungry, wild beasts and no way of escape.
Can human reasoning find anything good
in these circumstances?
I tell you, without Me, there's no hope,
but with Me nothing is hopeless.
I'm a God of miracles, and with Me
all things are possible.

You intended to harm me, but God intended it for good to accomplish
what is now being done, the saving of many lives.

GENESIS 50:20 NIV

February 6

Joseph, after suffering,
became Egypt's prime minister,
second in command of the entire civilized world.
Moses, following his forty-year
desert training program
became leader of his people
to the promised land
and father to the Jewish race.
Unpopular Daniel,
despised and thrown to lions,
became the highly honored
personal counselor to the king.
Think of yourself as if in training,
as these men were.
What will your spiritual training birth?
What will you become?

You should be strong. Don't give up,
because you will get a reward for your good work.

2 CHRONICLES 15:7 NCV

February 7

My disciples saw Me tortured on the cross.
They saw everything good
that I had brought from heaven
being murdered before their eyes.
They witnessed miracles, signs,
and wonders torn to pieces
and ruthlessly crucified.
They thought their hopes
were forever dashed.
They didn't know that My death
was the dawn of human hope.
I rose from the dead and released
My Spirit to them and to you.
The same Spirit that raised Me
from the dead lives in you.
You have the promise of all centuries
and universes living inside you.

God raised Jesus to life! And since God's Spirit of Resurrection
lives in you, he will also raise your dying body to life
by the same Spirit that breathes life into you!

ROMANS 8:11 TPT

February 8

I see all. I know all.
When you think things are falling apart,
remember I'm unshaken
by the storms of earth life.
I'm undeterred, unrattled, and undazed
by the problems that bother you.
I'm on My throne in heaven,
and I've ordained great things for you.
Don't be discouraged, ever.
I turn trouble into triumph.
Nothing can defeat you when
you have Me at your side.
Be strong today and let go of the things
that have been holding you down.

**Trust the Lord with all your heart,
and don't depend on your own understanding.**

PROVERBS 3:5 NCV

February 9

Today, dear one, I'm asking you
to pay special attention
to the words you speak.
Remember the tongue holds
tremendous power.
Life and death are in the power of the tongue.
Be very careful of gossip
or of speaking words that simply clutter
the air with noise.
Listen for the swirl
of angel breath around you.
Listen for the song of love
to overtake you, and then
begin to mimic what you hear.
Know that the words that you speak
birth eternal rewards, and the messages
of your heart produce life.

He who would love life and see good days,
let him refrain his tongue from evil,
and his lips from speaking deceit.

1 Peter 3:10 NKJV

February 10

I completely understand
when you're distressed,
but when you feel like giving up,
stop to think for a moment
about the price I paid for you.
It was a brutal death I suffered
on the cross so that your life
could be embraced with loving hope
and forgiveness.
I was crucified,
so that by My death you could receive
My Spirit to fill you and guide you.
Now, pause and listen.
Calm the roiling commotion in your heart,
and hear Me.
I have a great purpose for your life.
and we'll see you fulfill it together.

"Peace I leave with you; My peace I give to you;
not as the world gives do I give to you. Do not let your
heart be troubled, nor let it be fearful."

John 14:27 nasb

February 11

I've told you that without Me
you can do nothing, and it's true.
I'm your source for everything.
I see how hard you work.
I love your earnest heart and I love
your determination to help others.
I don't want you to burn out, though.
I don't want you to expend more
than I ask of you, and exhaust yourself
doing good.
Don't be afraid to pull back, to say no,
and to reduce your schedule
for more time to rest
and refresh yourself with Me.

**"I will personally go with you, Moses, and I will give you rest—
everything will be fine for you."**

Exodus 33:14 NLT

February 12

I've given you a path to travel
and I make you impenetrably strong
even when you don't think you are.
You're going to find
true happiness, joy, and fulfillment
on the path I've chosen for you,
(not one of your own making).
Stay close to Me, dear one, and know
that My Holy Spirit is busy guiding you.
Quiet your heart,
and turn your intention for the success
of this day and allow My Spirit
to do His beautiful work.

**You show me the path of life.
In your presence there is fullness of joy;
in your right hand are pleasures forevermore.**

PSALM 16:11 NRSV

February 13

Miracles will be a regular part
of your life from now on,
as you open the windows of your mind
to use the gifts I've given you.
The same faith that I've taught you
to use to climb a mountain
is teaching you
how to move mountains now.

"You don't have enough faith," Jesus told them.
"I tell you the truth, if you had faith even as small
as a mustard seed, you could say to this mountain,
'Move from here to there,' and it would move.
Nothing would be impossible."

MATTHEW 17:20 NLT

February 14

Goodness and mercy are following you
every day of your life.
I am the provider of all you need.
I am hope.
My hope is alive
inside you to encourage you
and move you forward
to your goals.
Be confident
of goodness surrounding you.
I know where you are
and where you're going because
I'm going with you.

Surely your goodness and love will follow me all the days of my life,
and I will dwell in the house of the LORD forever.

PSALM 23:6 NIV

February 15

I've called you to pray for others,
not only as a well-wisher,
but as a person of uncontested faith.
When you're confronted with sickness,
pray for healing, not just for blessing
and comfort.
I've told you to be My hands on the earth
to do the work I did.
In My name, child of Mine,
pray for the sick,
so they may be delivered, healed,
and blessed.

Are any among you sick? They should call for
the elders of the church and have them pray over them,
anointing them with oil in the name of the Lord.

JAMES 5:14 NRSV

February 16

I know the future.
Can you trust Me for the future?
I'm the author of hope,
and this hope lives in you.
As long as you're filled with
My presence, and as long as you're
filled with possibility,
you have hope.
The possibility of a better future
is what you hope for,
and I am that future.

May the God of hope fill you with all joy and peace in believing, that
you may abound in hope by the power of the Holy Spirit.

ROMANS 15:13 NKJV

February 17

I'm taking you from glory to glory every day,
bringing you closer to Me
and to the destiny you're called to.
Have faith for a beautiful
and fulfilling future
because great things are in store for you.
Today is a day to build confidence
in what I've already done for you
and what I'm presently doing for you.
Be thankful that you're alive
in this crucial hour.

We can all draw close to him with the veil removed from our faces.
And with no veil we all become like mirrors who brightly reflect the
glory of the Lord Jesus. We are being transfigured into his very image
as we move from one brighter level of glory to another. And this
glorious transfiguration comes from the Lord, who is the Spirit.

2 Corinthians 3:18 tpt

February 18

You won't understand who you are
by paying attention to your feelings,
which are fickle and untrustworthy.
Your feelings change from day to day
and moment to moment,
but what I say about you doesn't change.
You're My child, and I see you clearly
with all your emotions, thoughts,
talents, skills, desires, dreams, wants, needs–
nothing about you escapes My attention.
You have eternal life inside your veins,
so take your dignity and walk
with eternity in your step.

We do not lose heart. Even though our outward man is perishing, yet
the inward man is being renewed day by day. For our light affliction,
which is but for a moment, is working for us a far more exceeding and
eternal weight of glory, while we do not look at the things which are
seen, but at the things which are not seen. For the things which are
seen are temporary, but the things which are not seen are eternal.

2 Corinthians 4:16-18 nkjv

February 19

It's important for you to realize this day
that you have the nature and life of God in you.
The challenges before you will
require supernatural wisdom and
discernment, which I give to you liberally.
Use your spiritual gifts today
without hesitation.
Your faith will go before you
as you exercise My authority
in all situations.

It's time to be made new by every revelation that's been given to you.
And to be transformed as you embrace the glorious Christ-within as
your new life and live in union with him! For God has re-created you all
over again in his perfect righteousness, and you now belong to him in
the realm of true holiness.

EPHESIANS 4:23-24 TPT

February 20

I've created you perfectly,
body, soul, and spirit,
and your emotions are significant to Me.
But I tell you today, beware
of unbridled emotion that lands
in the lap of anger.
You'll produce nothing whatsoever of value
with anger.
Rise up with godly control and realize anger
is the result of feelings of powerlessness.
You are not powerless. I've given you
power, love, and a sound mind to look
at the world as I do–wisely.
Is an unruly temper wise?
No, it's devilish, so rise up strong;
resist the devil and watch him run.

"Don't sin by letting anger control you." Don't let the sun go down
while you're still angry, for anger gives a foothold to the devil.

EPHESIANS 4:26-27 NLT

February 21

In My kingdom there are no clocks.
Time does not rule in My kingdom.
When you allow time to limit you
by defining what you're capable of doing
or completing, you restrict My power in your life.
When you say words like, "it's too late,"
you snip the smile from the face of your future.
I created time to serve you, My child,
and I can multiply it for your use.
My mercy is new every morning,
and My grace knows no bounds.
Don't be controlled by time.
It is never too late.

The LORD's lovingkindnesses indeed never cease,
for His compassions never fail.
They are new every morning;
Great is Your faithfulness.

LAMENTATIONS 3:22-23 NASB

February 22

I'm a God of second chances.
Don't make excuses for stalling
or not going forward.
Ask Me for another chance.
Never be ashamed
to come to Me with an open, contrite
heart because I'm compassionate and
understanding, and I love you.
I understand when you grow weary,
and I want you to know I'm here to inspire
and re-kindle the hot flames
in your heart and soul.
Let Me ignite the fire of your passion
for the glorious life you're called to in Me.
There is nothing I can't turn around
and make better.

If we freely admit our sins when his light uncovers them,
he will be faithful to forgive us every time. God is just to
forgive us our sins because of Christ, and he will continue
to cleanse us from all unrighteousness.

1 John 1:9 TPT

February 23

I understand when you feel sorrow and pain.
On earth I was a man of sorrows
and acquainted with grief,
as it is written of Me.
I understand when you feel uncertainty and fear.
I understand loneliness and depression,
so today relinquish melancholy feelings to Me.
I can handle them.
Don't cling to gloomy emotions.
I'm here to rinse them with the life-giving power
of My blood, and to gloriously replenish
and renew your courage.

He was despised and rejected by men,
a man of deep sorrows who was no stranger
to suffering and grief.

ISAIAH 53:3 TPT

February 24

My love will never fail you.
I'll never run out on you and leave you
to fend for yourself.
I'll never betray you,
never take you for granted,
or take advantage of you.
I'll never walk away for someone else,
and I'll never promote someone else
in the job that belongs to you.
I'll never cheat you, steal from you,
or lie to you. I'll never call you a bad name
or put you down. Never!
Most of all, I'll never stop loving you.
With Me you have total and unquestioning
acceptance, appreciation, and permanence.
In Me, you are home. Your true home.
Don't accept the counterfeit.

God still loved us with such great love.
He is so rich in compassion and mercy.

EPHESIANS 2:4 TPT

February 25

What can you eliminate
from your busy schedule to free you up
for more time with Me?
Our moments together
are the most valuable moments of your day.
Don't be stingy with them.
I have much to share and enlighten you with,
and without our communication,
the world will quickly wear you out.
Make time today for Me so that
your soul and spirit can be refreshed.
I am the source of your inspiration,
not the world.
Your busy life will soon fade,
but your relationship with Me is forever.
Honor Me with your time today.

Come close to God, and God will come close to you.
Wash your hands, you sinners; purify your hearts,
for your loyalty is divided between God and the world.

JAMES 4:8 NLT

February 26

I'm never far from you.
As My mercy falls on you like rain.
Raise your heart to Me.
Praise Me in the shower. Lift your hands.
Every tear you cry I hold in My cup.
I never leave your side.
You won't stumble in the wind.
If your heart is storm-tossed, praise Me
in the tempest, and lift your eyes to the hills.
Where does your help come from?
Your help comes from Me,
the maker of heaven and earth.
I'm everything you need, sweetheart.
Everything you need
is right here inside you.

I look up to the mountains and hills, longing for God's help.
But then I realize that our true help and protection
come only from the Lord.

PSALM 121:1 TPT

February 27

I'm right here beside you
as I promised to be-forever.
I'm your comfort and your God.
I'm your redeemer. I save you from yourself
and from the devil who wants to eat you up.
You're nothing to him, and to Me
you're everything I love and care about.
All the visible world is sustained by the invisible,
so all your trials are like little Ferris wheels
in the transient traveling carnival of life.
Proclaim My promises out loud into the atmosphere.
Proclaim out loud what I've told you is yours.
Stop complaining about what you don't think
you have. Know and believe I've given you
everything you need. I'll always fulfill My promises
to you when you make a choice for Me
that means sacrifice to you.

**Just as we share abundantly in the sufferings of Christ,
so also our comfort abounds through Christ.**

2 CORINTHIANS 1:5 NIV

February 28

I want to answer your financial need today.
I want to unleash more tangible gifts upon you,
and in order to do as I desire,
you must be prepared.
Are you ready for a financial outpouring
of My favor? Are you willing
to persevere for your resources?
Prayer includes standing
and proclaiming that which is yours
knowing that you, and all you possess, are Mine.
Possess and live in the mansions
built by My values today.
My values don't include groveling,
giving up, or wringing of the hands.
My blessing over your life
brings riches without sorrow.
Believe this and understand your greatest wealth
is the wealth your soul possesses.

I will in the way of righteousness along the paths of justice,
bestowing a rich inheritance on those who love me
and making their treasuries full.

PROVERBS 8:20-21 NIV

MARCH

What then shall we say to these things?
If God is for us, who can be against us?

ROMANS 8:31 NKJV

March 1

Too often you take for granted
the glory that surrounds you.
Take time today to appreciate
and to love My presence in all things.
Look for Me in the small things.
Look for Me in the big things.
Look for Me in all things.
I'm in the wind blowing against your cheek.
I'm in the sun warming your neck.
I'm in the sweet kiss of morning
calling you to face the dawn,
and I'm in the glow of moonlight
as evening folds around you.
I'm in the exotic flavors of your favorite food,
and I'm in the beauty you love to embrace with your eyes.
I'm alive in your soul loving what you love.
Be very aware today that everything I've created
is for you.

O Lord, our God, no one can compare with you.
Such wonderful works and miracles are all found with you!
And you think of us all the time with your countless
expressions of love—far exceeding our expectations!

Psalm 40:5 tpt

March 2

I know your life has been difficult.
I know that you've had many hours
of loneliness and sadness, and I've been with you
every moment. I've caught each tear
in My holy bottle, but the tears of self-pity
have dropped by the wayside.
Selfish, self-centered self-woe
isn't inspired by My overcoming, all-powerful Spirit.
Darling child, here's what I want you to do:
reject the chains of self-pity and praise Me.
Praise Me through the trial.
Praise Me through all times of trouble.
I tell you, praise Me in absolutely everything!
Praise is the language of heaven,
and it's the language I want you to speak.
The grim spirit of heaviness will fall from you
as you enter into praise.
You'll begin to see the other side of suffering,
the bright flipside of sorrow.
Dance on your losses! Kick high and dance away!
I'll restore everything the devil has stolen from you.

You keep track of all my sorrows.
You have collected all my tears in your bottle.
You have recorded each one in your book.

PSALM 56:8 NLT

March 3

When I awaken you in the night
it's because I want to commune with you.
I don't wake you so you can turn on the TV
or play with your mobile device to smear
your soul with the world. I don't wake you
so you can check your email or raid the fridge,
or for any other reason the flesh might desire.
I wake you to for an important mission.
It's time to pray! You've been called
as a night watch intercessor. The night watch
is a crucial time of prayer and time to intercede.
My Holy Spirit will show you how to pray
and who and what to pray for. Rise up out of the bed
and pray, and when you return to your slumber,
I'll give you perfect peace and you'll wake up refreshed.
Not everyone is given this prayer mantle.
Take it seriously.

I have posted watchmen on your walls, Jerusalem;
they will never be silent day or night.
You who call on the LORD, give yourselves no rest.

ISAIAH 62:6 NIV

March 4

I'm calling you to learn My way
of thinking and talking.
I'm calling you to forsake your fleshly language
and hearken to the language I speak.
This takes listening. This takes being quiet
in My presence. This takes listening with
your entire heart and soul and spirit.
This takes putting yourself completely
into hearing the voice of love,
for this is the heart of My language.
I speak to you in symbols, metaphors,
and parables that only My children recognize.
If you want to understand what I'm saying,
you must learn to listen with your spiritual ears.
You must learn to think and talk the language
of My Spirit if you are to be fluent with My Word.

We speak about these things, not with words taught us by human
wisdom but with words taught us by the Spirit. And so we explain
spiritual truths to spiritual people.

1 CORINTHIANS 2:13 NCV

March 5

I want you to awaken
your body, mind, and heart
to this present moment.
I want you to sense My presence
embedded in your spirit.
When your heart and mind are quieted,
are you content to remain in the silence
for a while, or are you eager to return
to noise and your wild thoughts?
You're the one who controls
the matters of your heart.
You make the heart's choices.
Quiet your heart and sit
with Me a while, dear one;
sit with Me in stillness.

Be still, and know that I am God;
I will be exalted among the nations,
I will be exalted in the earth!

PSALM 46:10 NKJV

March 6

There's a time to sleep and a time to rise up.
Rise up, I say. Rise up from the slumber
that can overtake you in your waking hours.
You'll see things taking place in the world
that have never been seen before.
You'll see astonishing manifestations
in the heavens.
You'll see terrible things, acts of cruelty
and human devastation.
You'll see Bible prophecy unfold
before your eyes.
This is not a time to sleep.
Wake, I say; wake, and be consumed
with faith and the knowledge of My will.
This is no time to sleep.

I will show wonders in the heavens above
and signs on the earth below, blood and fire
and billows of smoke.

ACTS 2:19 NIV

March 7

Listen with the eyes of your heart
and hear with the ears of your heart.
Watch and listen for the undercurrents
of My Spirit moving in you and around you.
Fix your gaze on Me so you don't miss
the messages I'm bringing you today.
Look around you and you'll see Me
at work in a million ways
you haven't been aware of.
Faith consists not in seeing miracles,
but in seeing miracles with new eyes.

Your lovingkindness is before my eyes,
and I have walked in Your truth.

PSALM 26:3 NASB

March 8

If you're going to catch the move of My Spirit,
take inventory of doing the same old things
the same old way, thinking the same old thoughts
and acting out the same old safe behavior patterns.
If you're going to bring the fresh wind
of My presence into your life,
step out on a limb in My Spirit,
and move out of the fleshy, risk-proof
habits that shun challenge and danger.
A vibrant life of faith includes surprise,
discovery, wonder, and yes–danger.
Spice up your faith today, beloved,
and choose to follow Me wherever I lead,
even if it's out on a limb.
Don't imprison My Spirit in the locked rooms
of the same old way.

If anyone is in Christ, he is a new creature;
the old things passed away;
behold, new things have come.

2 CORINTHIANS 5:17 NASB

March 9

It's time to be fully alert and aware
in the world. On the night before
My crucifixion, in the Garden of Gethsemane
after My final meal with My disciples,
I asked them to watch and pray with Me.
I knew My fate and wanted them
to stay alert and pray. They fell asleep.
Perhaps they couldn't face
what was about to happen,
but I tell you that when you resist the truth
of an experience, you'll fall asleep
to the truth and what's real.
You might not like the events of the world,
but I tell you, remain alert so nothing escapes
your spiritual attention.
Keep your prayer antenna ever up
and ready for action. I'm calling you
to stay alert and pray.

"Are you asleep? Couldn't you keep watch for one hour?
Watch and pray so that you will not fall into temptation.
The spirit is willing, but the flesh is weak."

MARK 14:37-38 NIV

March 10

When you allow Me to be Lord of your life
and your faculties are awakened to Me,
you begin to be aware of places
in your life where you've become
hard-hearted. There are so many parts
of yourself you try to protect from pain
or disappointment, and without realizing it,
both your body and mind become hardened.
You can become inflexible in your thinking,
and past experiences can become walls of concrete
to keep you from grasping future possibilities.
Don't let your mind become hardened against others
because of limited and damaged vision.
Darling child, I'll remove the heart of stone from you
and give you My heart. I want to awaken in you
the sacred move of My Spirit who speaks across
every barrier you've set up to deny yourself happiness.
I will teach you to respect me completely, and I will put a
new way of thinking inside you. I will take out the stubborn
hearts of stone from your bodies, and I will give you obedient
hearts of flesh.

I will teach you to respect me completely, and I will put a new way of
thinking inside you. I will take out the stubborn hearts of stone from
your bodies, and I will give you obedient hearts of flesh.

EZEKIEL 36:26 NCV

March 11

Trust Me to know
exactly what you need.
It's not a self-serving, easy-breezy life
that your precious soul craves,
but the glory of a profound spiritual adventure
surrendered to Me.
When you stay chained
to your sofa with your brain captive to worldly TV
and your heart snared by temptations of every lurid sort,
how do you suppose you'll rise up full of holy zing
and My joy?
I live at the deep root of your being.
Today, enter the urgent spaces of your heart
where I'll come to speak and guide you.

Take a lesson from the ants, you lazybones.
Learn from their ways and become wise!

PROVERBS 6:6 NLT

March 12

Today is a day to trust Me.
I know that things have been difficult for you.
I know how hard you've been working,
and I'm asking you to trust Me and know
that I'm guiding and leading you
into a wonderful place where you're going to
receive more than what you've asked for.
This is not the time to give up.
When you trust Me for rewards
and payment for your labors,
you escape a million sorrows and frustrations.
Not only that, you'll have a feeling of holy expectation.
This feeling is one of delight.
I want you to experience delight
in your soul as you're being fed
by My Holy Spirit. Stay strong,
and praise Me in this time of spiritual growth.

We honor them as our heroes because they remained faithful even while enduring great sufferings. And you have heard of all that Job went through and we can now see that the Lord ultimately treated him with wonderful kindness, revealing how tenderhearted he really is!

JAMES 5:11 TPT

March 13

Breathe in the air and feel the breath of God
fill your lungs. Know that you're never alone.
I'm strengthening your body now.
I know that you've been working hard
and that you're tired.
I'm toughening you and adding
new vigor to you even now.
This is not a time to throw in the towel
and give up. The storm is ending
and you're going to see beautiful rays
of light shining on your situation
because I've proclaimed it.
I've watched you grow
and I've watched you
as you've stood strong.
I salute you and I say to you,
"Well done, My good and faithful servant."

"Well done, my good and faithful servant. You have been faithful
in handling this small amount, so now I will give you many more
responsibilities. Let's celebrate together!"

MATTHEW 25:21 NLT

March 14

Let Me show you a better way.
When you stress out and become nervous
and worry, use the glory of the moment entirely.
It's not the work that counts as much as
your attitude and your heart as you do the work.
I've called you for a special task,
and you'll accomplish that task perfectly.
You'll accomplish it because
I'm with you and in you. Your true occupation
is to walk by My Spirit in all things
that you do and encounter in your life.
If you hang a bird feeder out your window
and the birds fly around it and avoid eating from it,
what's the point of the feeder?
If I hold out to you all the spiritual nourishment you need
to overcome the cares of life and you fall into
pits of despair, ignoring what I offer,
what good is My nourishment?
Do not mock God, dear one.
Cherish your holy calling.

Do not be deceived; God is not mocked,
for you reap whatever you sow.

Galatians 6:7 nrsv

March 15

This day
I want you to allow My Holy Spirit
to flood through your being
so that everything you do
and touch is stress-free.
Even sickness can bring you
enormous stress.
I want you free
from the stress of all impairments,
body, soul, and spirit.
I'll endow you with grace and power,
and I'll adorn you with the clothing
of spiritual authority
to step into heaven's living room
with peace in your heart.

**The mind governed by the flesh is death,
but the mind governed by the Spirit is life and peace.**

ROMANS 8:6 NIV

March 16

Today, pay attention to your diet.
Examine the food that you eat
and think about its value to your bones,
muscles, tissues, the cells of your brain,
and your entire being.
Plan the food that you'll eat
to nourish the body in which I dwell.
Your body belongs to Me.
It's My temple, My palace,
My home sweet home.
Make sure that you feel good
and that you feel strong and capable
of carrying your body into the world
with integrity and vigor.
Exercise and be strong for Me.

Do you not know that your body is a temple of the Holy Spirit
who is in you, whom you have from God, and that you
are not your own? For you have been bought with a price:
therefore glorify God in your body.

1 Corinthians 6:19-20 nasb

March 17

Be sure you nourish your soul.
Nourish your soul with friends
of like mind and spirit.
Don't neglect friendships
where you can pray together
and storm heaven with the fire
of My Spirit. Encourage one another!
Seek out leaders and teachers
who'll help to bring you to a higher level
of faith. Seek out and pursue spiritual
teachers who challenge you to stretch and reach out
for more of Me. You need friends and relationships
that inspire and nourish you in My Spirit
to keep you from becoming complacent.
Look around you. Who inspires and challenges you?
Why do you surround yourself
with oppressive influences?
I called you to walk inspired.

**Let us think of ways to motivate one another
to acts of love and good works.**

HEBREWS 10:24 NLT

March 18

There's wisdom in walking away from
certain things that are finished.
Don't hold onto things that you think are good
when they're not.
There are certain things that appear to be right,
but they aren't right.
Know for certain that the choices you make
are My choices. Don't be deceived by your own
fleshly feelings, for the flesh is huge,
and it can crowd out the power and the wisdom
of My Spirit in your spirit. Let go today of everything
that you know is not of Me and you'll see
an outpouring of glory take place in your life.
Don't be afraid of the new and the unknown,
for I promise you that it will be exciting
and bring you much happiness.

God has united you with Christ Jesus. For our benefit God made him
to be wisdom itself. Christ made us right with God; he made us pure
and holy, and he freed us from sin.

1 CORINTHIANS 1:30 NLT

March 19

I've blessed you with a great blessing
that's upon you as a living force,
and this force of blessing
will never leave you. I have blessed you.
Only that which is of the flesh
can stand in the way of My blessing.
The flesh hinders and interrupts the flow
of My blessing, but your spirit is stronger
than your flesh when you exercise it rigorously.
Why exercise the body when it's your spirit
that needs the most exercise?
When you exercise the body, make sure
that your spirit is exercised even more.
My Spirit infused with your spirit
overcomes the greediness of the flesh,
and My blessing then overtakes you
in every area of your life.
As you yield freely and fully to the dynamic life
and power of the Holy Spirit,
you will abandon the cravings of your self-life.

As you yield freely and fully to the dynamic life and power of the Holy
Spirit, you will abandon the cravings of your self-life.

GALATIANS 5:16 TPT

March 20

When you're faced with a situation
where you don't know what to do,
is it because you feel you don't have
adequate resources to make a decision?
Let Me remind you, you have My mind.
I'll direct you and lead you if you'll take your mind off
what you don't have and look at what you do have.
I'll help you take the first little step toward the unknown
when you don't know what to do.
When I healed the paralytic at the Pool of Bethesda,
I didn't tell him to get up and train for a marathon.
I said, "Rise, take up your mat and walk,"
and I'm telling you the same. Take that first step
into the unknown. I never sit twiddling My fingers
with My mind confused wondering what to do next.
I am a God of action, and because I live inside your spirit
by My Holy Spirit, the answers are within you.
Act on what you know and what you believe.
Look at what you have in Me. And take that step.

"Who has known the mind of the Lord? Who has been able to teach
him?" But we have the mind of Christ.

1 CORINTHIANS 2:16 NCV

March 21

Invite your body to worship Me
in your physical exercise.
Your body and your breath will feed your mind
and your soul into spiritual awareness.
Sometimes you think that exercise
is separate from your spiritual life.
I say take Me into your body and exercise!
Stretch and grow strong in My Spirit
as you worship Me with every muscle,
tissue, and fiber of your body.
In the silent spaces of your work-out,
healing will take place
because your body is holy,
and exercise is your holy tool.
You live in your body and your body is Mine.

Whether you eat or drink, or whatever you do,
do all to the glory of God.

1 CORINTHIANS 10:31 ESV

March 22

What would happen if you allowed yourself
to be vulnerable today? I've called you
to walk with Me, and that means
I direct the path. Let Me direct the path.
You only arrive where I'm going
if you walk there with Me.
You can't take a bus or an airplane
to get where I'm going
if I'm not operating the bus and the airplane.
Walk with Me, for this is a profound practice for you.
You're being led to let go of your own agenda
and discover which direction I'm going in.
Don't be afraid of the unknown.
This is a practice of profound trust in Me.
Come along and let's walk.

**Blessed are those who trust in the LORD
and have made the LORD their hope and confidence.**

JEREMIAH 17:7 NLT

March 23

Expect a move of My Spirit
in your family.
You've prayed and I'm answering
your prayers.
My blessing is upon you
and upon your house.
I keep My covenant
with My own who love Me
to a thousand generations.
I heal and I bless.
I restore and I embrace
with My love.

Know therefore that the LORD your God is God; he is the faithful God,
keeping his covenant of love to a thousand generations of those who
love him and keep his commandments.

DEUTERONOMY 7:9 NIV

March 24

I'm stretching you and giving you
a divine opportunity to trust Me in you.
I don't treat you like a machine expecting you
to get out there and do impossible things on your own.
No, I've called you to take part in what I'm doing.
If there are things in your life
you feel are simply too big for you to accomplish,
or if you think you're inadequate,
remind yourself that you can do all things
through Me because I give you the aptitude
and the strength.
With Me nothing is impossible for you.

I can do all things through Christ who strengthens me.
PHILIPPIANS 4:13 NKJV

March 25

I listen when My children pray.
Think about these things quietly as you go to bed
and as you rise up in the morning.
Do what's right and trust Me completely.
I turn shame into honor.
I'll make you happier
than you ever could've dreamed of being
without Me.
You can go to bed and sleep
in peace because I'm right here loving you.
I'm blessing you
with all spiritual blessings.
My blessings are endless.

When you lie down, you will not be afraid;
when you lie down, your sleep will be sweet.

PROVERBS 3:24 NIV

March 26

Tell Me what you need every morning
knowing I'll answer every need.
Because of your sweet love for Me,
it's a joy to answer you.
I love to show you the right thing to do.
and how I want you to live
because you listen.
You bring Me much pleasure,
My love;
ask and keep on asking.

For the LORD takes delight in his people;
He crowns the humble with victory.

PSALM 149:4 NIV

March 27

Every morning
when you awake, I'm there beside you.
I hear you and I have mercy on you
at all times: when you're weak
and when you're strong.
I hear you.
I know when your bones ache
and your energy wanes.
I know when you laugh wildly
and when your pillow is wet with tears.
I see you in triumph and in defeat.
Never doubt Me.
I'm your miracle, your trophy,
your fortune, and your strength.
I'm the fuel and hope
you need, dear one, not the world.

"Be strong and courageous. Do not be afraid
or terrified because of them, for the LORD your God
goes with you; he will never leave you nor forsake you."

DEUTERONOMY 31:6 NIV

March 28

Nothing is too damaged for Me
to repair.
Nothing is too broken
that I can't put together again.
Nothing can go too far away from Me
that I can't find it.
Nothing is too weak
that I can't make strong.
Rise up today,
dear one, and take what you need
from Me.
I want to give you everything.

What a glorious God!
He gives us salvation over and over,
then daily he carries our burdens!

PSALM 68:19 TPT

March 29

Be kind to My servants.
Honor your pastors, your teachers.
The seat of scorn
is lined with needles and thorns.
To find fault, complain, or fuss in your heart
about your leaders will only dig holes
into your flesh, and you'll attract
more thorns and needles.
Remember, like attracts like.
Your complaints attract more complaining,
and soon you'll forget how to bless.
Blessing and curses can't occupy
the same space in your heart.
Honor, bless, and pray for your leaders.
I'll do the rest.

Make sure that you show your deep appreciation for those who cherish
you and diligently work as ministers among you. For they are your
leaders who care for you, teach you, and stand before the Lord on
your behalf. They value you with great love. Because of their service to
you, let peace reign among yourselves.

1 Thessalonians 5:12-13 tpt

March 30

If you dwell on
what you're afraid of,
you build a continent of fear
in your mind until the truth
stands outside your heart,
knocking with no one answering.
The voice of fear is a foul stench
in the sweet garden of faith.
Resist fear at all cost.
Never be afraid.
Let yourself bloom and blossom
in the ecstasy of trust today.
I won't fail you.
I promise.

"Don't ever be afraid, dearest friends! Your loving Father joyously gives
you his kingdom realm with all its promises!"

Luke 12:32 TPT

March 31

How much of your thinking is focused on the past?
How much on the future?
Can you rest a moment,
and be completely here with Me now?
Come; sit here with Me for a moment.
We won't talk; we'll just sit together.
Allow your body to relax;
take a deep breath and be with Me.
Just be.
This may be difficult for you to do
because you're so accustomed to focusing
on events and issues that have already taken place,
or those things which are in the future.
For now, at this moment,
as it comes to the end of the month,
simply sit with Me in stillness,
as My Spirit performs a new work in your heart.

We don't remember what happened in the past, and in future
generations, no one will remember what we are doing now.

ECCLESIASTES 1:11 NLT

APRIL

"If the Son makes you free,

you shall be free indeed."

JOHN 8:36 NKJV

April 1

Give your blessing to your past, present and future.
Send grace and love to the cells of your body.
Send faith and hope to your thought patterns.
Within you is the power that created the universe!
Today, come against the lies
of hopelessness and powerlessness
that you've entertained.
Consider the root cause of the negative thinking.
The feeling of hopelessness is a close relative
to powerlessness.
Think about this for a moment.
What do you have power over?
Guilt, fear, shame, and depression fester
in misplaced feelings of hopelessness
and powerlessness. These are the feelings
that are at the root of your negative thinking.
You're never powerless!

I admit that I haven't yet acquired the absolute fullness
that I'm pursuing, but I run with passion into his abundance
so that I may reach the purpose that Jesus Christ has called me
to fulfill and wants me to discover.

PHILIPPIANS 3:12 TPT

April 2

Today, when you feel powerless,
remember that you have within you
all the power you need
through My Holy Spirit.
Oh how My children limit
themselves by forgetting their power!
Never limit Me, and never limit
the power of My Holy Spirit in you.
Tell yourself the truth today.
You have the power to overcome temptation,
the power to change your life,
the power to be healed, the power to forgive,
the power to achieve and go forward fearlessly!
You have the power to see My promises come alive
in your life and the lives of those you pray for.
Have a serious talk with yourself about the power
I've given you, and choose to walk in your power!

"You will receive power when the Holy Spirit has come
upon you; and you will be my witnesses in Jerusalem,
in all Judea and Samaria, and to the ends of the earth."

ACTS 1:8 NRSV

April 3

Today, open your heart to be grateful
for the myriad angels watching over you.
You're not alone,
even when you think you are.
When trouble multiplies around you,
your angels are there to lift you up
out of danger, destruction, and despair.
My angels are light and happy
and they surround you
with their heavenly character and power.
You're equipped to go through
any trouble with your banner of faith
marching before you.
So today, be comforted.
Angels are at your side cheering you on.

He has put his angels in charge of you
to watch over you wherever you go.
They will catch you in their hands so that you
will not hit your foot on a rock.

PSALM 91:11-12 NCV

April 4

Today, look around you
to see who you can bless.
Who can you be
My instrument of blessing to?
Someone needs your kindness
and your generosity.
Someone needs
the tender attention
only you can give.
Find them.

"Give, and you will receive. Your gift will return to you
in full—pressed down, shaken together to make room for more,
running over, and poured into your lap. The amount you give will
determine the amount you get back."

LUKE 6:38 NLT

April 5

I want you to realize that what I give you
is better than life.
The wisdom and knowledge
I give you is the thrill of every lifetime.
The miracles that I've given you
to perform are more exciting
beyond any human endeavor.
I give you eyes to see that which is unseen.
I give you ears to hear that which is unheard.
I've given you My breath to breathe,
and My heart to pump new life into yours.
Rejoice, today, My child.
You have it all.

Because Your lovingkindness is better than life,
My lips shall praise You.

PSALM 63:3 NKJV

April 6

I'm your constant friend.
I watch over you and have every hair
on your head accounted for.
How much more do I care
about your thoughts and your happiness?
I've delivered you from
the past and set you loose from shame.
I've kissed away every tear,
and I'm here now to take your hand
and walk you into a beautiful new phase
of your life. Think with your
renewed mind, darling,
and let happiness overtake you.

"Why, even the hairs of your head are all numbered.
Fear not; you are of more value than many sparrows."

LUKE 12:7 ESV

April 7

Don't worry.
Your tasks will be completed
one at a time and your life
will fulfill all that I set before you.
You'll see everything fulfilled
sequentially, in perfect order
and with success. I don't want you fatigued
with concern over things you can't control.
Know that when you give the tasks to Me
and rest in My abilities, trusting Me,
you'll be much happier.
Other people are blessed
by the infectious spirit of happiness
you exude through Me.
What you do, dear one,
is important, yes, but not as important
as who you are to Me.

"What appears humanly impossible is more than possible with God.
For God can do what man cannot."

LUKE 18:27 TPT

April 8

Be free of social constraints today.
Let My grace within you
carry your compassion and caring
to the world around you.
You'll be amazed at the rich rewards
that encompass you as the day unfolds.
Each of your personal connections
have meaning,
and I am smiling with you
as a fresh wind of blessing sweeps over your
social life.

"If the Son sets you free, you are truly free."

JOHN 8:36 NLT

April 9

The more you know of Me,
the more revelation
of My bountiful favor you have.
You've been in possession of My favor
since you surrendered your life to Me,
and I want you to understand
that My favor is centered in purpose.
I've called you to walk in the light
of My love and guidance, and to bask
in the joy of My unending favor
because your life has purpose.
Good things are ahead for you today.
Reach out for all that I have for you.
You're surrounded by love.

"I have raised you up for this very purpose, that I might show you my
power and that my name might be proclaimed in all the earth."

Exodus 9:16 NIV

April 10

When it seems like you're stuck
in a hopeless situation,
humble yourself, and ask Me
for wisdom.
When you feel like you can't–
know that I can!
I want to help you to overcome
and prevail in all situations!
My Holy Spirit will guide you
as you confront upcoming challenges.
Take wisdom as your chief weapon,
and your challenges
will shrink to dust.

Humble yourselves in the sight of the Lord, and He will lift you up.

JAMES 4:10 NKJV

April 11

Today, walk with Me
and show kindness to someone,
even if you think they don't deserve
kindness.
Show mercy and act with justice.
This is a day
to humble yourself and demonstrate
to others My goodness that lives in you.
Love Me and serve Me
with your entire mind, heart, and being.
I give you these directions for your good
because you're precious to Me.

He has shown you, O mortal, what is good.
And what does the LORD require of you?
To act justly and to love mercy and to walk humbly with your God.

MICAH 6:8 NIV

April 12

When you pray
and then seem to wait forever
for an answer,
understand that My wisdom
often holds back the answers you wait for.
Not getting what you want at the moment
can be a divine blessing. Sometimes
the problems that you face are gifts
from Me for you to solve,
and in your solving them,
you advance up the ladder
of dynamic faith.
I want you to walk
in wisdom and recognize the amazing
power you possess within you.
Wisdom makes all the difference.
I always answer.

He who gets wisdom loves his own soul;
He who keeps understanding will find good.

PROVERBS 19:8 NASB

April 13

When I spoke to Job after listening
to his complaints, I asked him
if he knew more of My purposes than I knew;
was he more wise than I, the creator of
heaven and earth?
Job's heart broke before Me
as he cried that he'd change his heart and his life.
I tell you, because of Job's humility
and his heart of true praise and worship,
I multiplied his blessings, and blessed
the last of his life more than the first.
I want to multiply your blessings, too.
See Me for who I am; worship and praise
the one who knows all and is all.
You'll grow in success
and let Me multiply your blessings.

You will experience all these blessings if you obey the LORD your God.

DEUTERONOMY 28:2 NLT

April 14

When you act in faith believing
in My faithful promises and help,
you increase the substance
of your faith.
Your faith becomes increased with use.
Your assignment is to take
what I've given you
and use it in your daily life.
Allow your faith
to grow and grow and grow.
Especially today.
Let Me see your acts of faith today
because I'm giving you all you need.

Prove to me that you have faith without works and
I will show you faith by my works as proof that I believe.

JAMES 2:18 TPT

April 15

I love your heart
because you have a kind heart.
I love how you reach out to help someone
when no one's looking.
I love the way you have a smile for strangers.
I love how you can make a person
feel good about themselves,
and give a kind word when it's
not called for, and
I love it when you show kindness
even when you don't feel like it.
Know today that I observe all;
nothing escapes My eye.

When you demonstrate generosity, do it with pure motives and
without drawing attention to yourself.

MATTHEW 6:3 TPT

April 16

Don't be taken advantage of.
I've told you to turn the other cheek,
but I also tell you to rise up and be strong,
and stand for that which you know is right.
Stop the oppressor in his tracks.
Say no to what appears outwardly
to be good, but inwardly you're fully aware
that it's not good.
Beloved, I'm not an in-between God,
or an almost-Jesus. There's no
somewhat-Christian or maybe-Holy
at work here.
Know that My eye goes to and fro
throughout the entire world searching
for the one who's genuinely true to Me.
You can't be foolish and wise at the same time.
Allow My wisdom
to dictate all your actions today.

Be of good courage, and let us be strong for our people and for the
cities of our God. And may the Lord do what is good in His sight.

2 Samuel 10:12 nkjv

April 17

Breathe in this moment.
See the moments I give you
as holy gifts because
I breathe in your breath.
You're My eyes in this moment.
You're My ears in this moment.
You're My hands in this moment.
Every breath you take is a treasure.
Whenever you start to complain, stop!
Beware of fault-finding and
feeding the crows of discontent.
Enjoy your life right now.
I've given you everything.

**"I will forget my complaint, I will put off my sad face,
and be of good cheer."**

JOB 9:27 ESV

April 18

I've given you the gift of creativity
in all things. You're creative in your work,
your finances and your relationships.
Trust your creative heart to reach into
situations and create good.
Don't be afraid to take chances today.
Step out in faith to depart from doing things
the usual way, or what you call ordinary.
I've created inside you abilities
that are extraordinary and beyond
your human strength and wisdom.
Take a chance today–take that step of faith
and watch Me work.

Faith is confidence in what we hope for
and assurance about what we do not see.

HEBREWS 11:1 NIV

April 19

Think of yourself starting a race.
You're at the starting line,
and you're off and running
with the course ahead of you.
I see you at the finish line, dear one.
I'm with you at the starting line
empowering you, cheering you on,
and I'm also at the finish line
with My arms out celebrating your win.
Be joyful today with the knowledge
that I'm with you every inch of the way,
and I'm very pleased with you.

As for us, we have all of these great witnesses who encircle us like clouds. So we must let go of every wound that has pierced us and the sin we so easily fall into. Then we will be able to run life's marathon race with passion and determination, for the path has been already marked out before us.

HEBREWS 12:1 TPT

April 20

Stay calm when bedlam breaks loose
around you. Hold onto your peace.
Hold on tight and let the storm rage on
as you sit calmly content, knowing I'm in control,
and I'll work out every detail perfectly
on your behalf. You're called to rise above
the blizzards of discontent.
When disappointment rains on your plans,
duck into the safety of My shelter.
Discontent will cloud your faith and open
the floodgates for showers of muddy self-pity
to blacken the hope I've set before you.
Stay strong, dear one. You're never alone.
You're important in the spirit realm,
which is your true habitation.
You're alive in the world with a body and soul,
but your spirit is a citizen of heaven,
where you're alive and highly-favored forever.

The LORD will fight for you, and you shall hold your peace.

EXODUS 14:14 NKJV

April 21

Sing to Me your new song
with the harmonies and rhythms
I'm giving you.
Write the lyrics in the native language
of your heart.
Listen for your music in the night hours
and wake to it in your ears.
The earth trembles at the sound
of heaven's song–
My gift to you.

Sing to the LORD a new song;
sing to the LORD, all the earth.

PSALM 96:1 NIV

April 22

I'm greater than your soul;
therefore, I alone can satisfy
your longings and desires.
You won't find lasting
happiness in the swoop of the world's
giddy Ferris wheel of delights.
You'll soon lose what you thought
was yours. Remain solid with Me.
I've told you I'm the truth,
and when you think of Me,
think of that.
I am all there is of the truth,
not merely a part of truth.
I'm all truth. Meditate on this.
Cherish things I've given you to love today.
Rejoice in the blessings I give you
through loved ones.

**He satisfies the longing soul,
and the hungry soul he fills with good things.**

PSALM 107:9 ESV

April 23

Your hands are blessed today.
I've noticed how you use your hands,
how you love with your hands.
I'm removing every spec of yesterday's dust
from the flesh of your hands
and you're going to go forward
with clean hands to do great works
for Me—only for Me.

Have you not put a fence around him and his house and all that he has, on every side? You have blessed the work of his hands, and his possessions have increased in the land.

JOB 1:10 NRSV

April 24

When people cut you off,
don't give it a second thought.
I am the Lord.
I pick you up in My arms
where you're always at home.
You're never cut off from Me.
Reach the mountaintop today!
If you stumble,
don't pause for a second,
and don't lie down in the thorns
feeling sorry for yourself.
Rise up and continue on;
I'm building your spiritual muscles.
My chosen mountain climbers
are Holy Spirit athletes.

**He gives prosperity to the poor
and protects those who suffer.**

JOB 5:11 NLT

April 25

What things do you accept in your life
that you know aren't okay?
It's not okay to be trampled on
and misused.
Let your heart do the walking
from such things, I say.
Walk quickly from all that wounds
what I love.
I'm here to create all things new for you.
All things. Not just one or two things in your life,
but all things. When you wake
in the morning, open your eyes to a new day.
All things are new.
Wake up,
and take the good life I give you!

Turn away from evil and do good.
Search for peace, and work to maintain it.

Psalm 34:14 NLT

April 26

I make it possible for all humanity
to receive the fullness of God.
My Holy Spirit has empowered you
to carry out the purposes of God.
I've sent you My Spirit
to constantly remind you
that I'm faithful.
You're the promise of the Father,
and you're empowered to carry
My fullness into the world.
Go.
You take My heart with you.

"Go into all the world and preach the gospel to all creation."
MARK 16:15 NIV

April 27

I want you to bring Me
into your life in a deeper way today.
I've told you to seek first
My kingdom
above all else and it should be
your most earnest pursuit.
I'm showing you how to experience
this on an everyday basis
because I want you to have a clearer
understanding of the relationship
between your human spirit
and My Holy Spirit.
I want you to enjoy sweet intimacy
with Me, the lover of your soul,
every day.

Seek first the kingdom of God and His righteousness,
and all these things shall be added to you.

MATTHEW 6:33 NKJV

April 28

Far beyond
rules and formulas and dictates,
I want to be your focus of attention
and the chief desire of your heart.
Keep your mind set on things
that are above, not beneath.
I'm helping you to be more aware
of heavenly realities than your
present circumstances today.
I'm showing you how to work through
the problems that you have in front of you.
I am your everything, and I am your partner
in everything you're facing.

**Set your mind on the things above,
not on the things that are on earth.**

COLOSSIANS 2:3 NASB

April 29

You haven't been given a spirit of fear,
but of power, love, and a sound mind!
Fear gives the enemy access
to your thought life.
He has no right to that access.
Keep your mind fixed
on My goodness and love.
It's My love that casts out all fear
from your mind.
Speak My words
which I've taught you, and the devil will
run from you.

Love never brings fear, for fear is always related to punishment.
But love's perfection drives the fear of punishment
far from our hearts. Whoever walks
constantly afraid of punishment has
not reached love's perfection.

1 John 4:18 tpt

April 30

Pray today for My Holy Spirit
to teach you how to declare
the truth in your daily life.
My Holy Spirit is your helper
and your comforter.
Understand today that you can move heaven
with your faith.
You are empowered to do as I did on the earth.
You are not My employee,
you're My co-laborer.

"No longer do I call you slaves, for the slave does not know what his master is doing; but I have called you friends, for all things that I have heard from My Father I have made known to you. You did not choose Me but I chose you, and appointed you that you would go and bear fruit, and that your fruit would remain, so that whatever you ask of the Father in My name He may give to you."

JOHN 15:15-16 NASB

MAY

Arise, shine;

For your light has come!

And the glory of the LORD

is risen upon you.

ISAIAH 60:1 NKJV

May 1

Make this a month of creative thinking.
Let your creative juices flow.
Reach out from the ordinary
into the extraordinary,
and rise and shine.
Reach out and take from Me
the energy that'll accomplish more
than you expect in your circumstances.
Discover the fullness of living
in unexplored places,
and trust your instincts.
I'm with you and I enjoy you.

Cry out for comprehension and intercede for insight. For if you keep seeking it like a man would seek for sterling silver, searching in hidden places for cherished treasure, then you will discover the fear of the Lord and find the true knowledge of God.

PROVERBS 2:3-5 TPT

May 2

You're being loved right now
and you've found forever with Me.
Let Me encourage you.
You're beautiful to Me.
I want you to succeed.
Believe and be strong today.

Depend on the LORD in whatever you do,
and your plans will succeed.

PROVERBS 16:3 NCV

May 3

Be filled with hope today
because you're on your way.
You've just begun your journey!
When you look around
with an envious, competitive eye,
and compare yourself to others,
you'll upset yourself foolishly.
Keep your eye on Me only.
Love Me and I'll show you greater things
than you've known, and I'll take you
places no one else has been.

A heart at peace gives life to the body,
but envy rots the bones.

PROVERBS 14:30 NIV

May 4

This is a day
for you to move forward
You're not alone. Be brave.
Don't be side-tracked;
stay on course.
Follow the strategy
you've worked on,
for all is good
and will bring forth
much fruit and blessing.

I do not consider myself yet to have taken hold of it.
But one thing I do: Forgetting what is behind
and straining toward what is ahead.

PHILIPPIANS 3:13 NIV

May 5

Don't allow yourself to be upset
over trivial things.
Many things that are inconsequential
loom up before you
and steal your energy
and your attention.
Let them go.
Give your attention
to that which is essential.
I've given you the gift
of wisdom to employ at all times.
Rise up and be wise today.

Christ's resurrection is your resurrection too.
This is why we are to yearn for all that is above,
for that's where Christ sits enthroned at the place of
all power, honor, and authority! Yes, feast on all the treasures
of the heavenly realm and fill your thoughts with heavenly realities,
and not with the distractions of the natural realm.

COLOSSIANS 3:1-2 TPT

May 6

I'm your courage and your source
of power and energy.
When you feel depleted and tired,
I'll renew your strength.
The world has never given you
what you've craved and needed,
but I'm here for you to help you
become all you can be today.
Be invigorated with new insight, faith,
and resolve from My storehouse
of inspiration.
Renewed with strength,
you'll be a hero, and you're going to change
your circumstances.
You bless the godly, O Lord;
you surround them with your shield of love.

**You bless the godly, O Lord;
you surround them with your shield of love.**

Psalm 5:12 nlt

May 7

If you need more patience today,
ask Me and I'll ignite your faith
and fire up your soul with renewed
and enduring patience. It takes courage
to be patient, and I'll cover you in
a warm cloak of patience if you'll let Me.
Oh, be brave today, dear one, and have
fun. You'll be a lot more patient when
you stop taking yourself so seriously.
Everything you do is under My careful eye,
so let patience have its perfect work.
This is a good day.

Let patience have its perfect work,
that you may be perfect and complete,
lacking nothing.

JAMES 1:4 NKJV

May 8

You never lose anything forever
when you're Mine. I'm a giving God
and I give back. When you lose something,
possessions, position, money, identity,
or a loved one, there's a tearing away
inside that happens, and it's then
that you're faced with what really
counts in your life. I want to hold you
in My arms every day and assure your
heart that all is well, and I want to lead
you to new horizons of possibilities.
I want to show you paths of freedom
where discovery and delight brighten
the way ahead. Don't focus on what
you've lost, but rekindle the fire for
loving the essence of all life
in your walk with Me.

**Whatever things were gain to me,
those things I have counted as loss
for the sake of Christ.**

PHILIPPIANS 3:7 NASB

May 9

Today, you're going to experience faith
in greater measure.
You're going to feel secure
knowing I'm your God,
your forever, faithful friend.
You're safe in Me and free
from fear or doubt.
Yes, I've called you
to dark places where faith
in Me is but a dim, flickering
candle wick.
Be confident, sweetheart.
Don't waiver.
You shine with the light of heaven.

**He uncovers the deeps out of darkness,
and brings deep darkness to light.**

JOB 12:22 NRSV

May 10

Today, marks a special day
for you to recognize who you are in Me.
Don't think for a moment that your work is finished.
You're about to take off on a spiritual adventure
that'll shake your world.
I'm calling you to a higher place,
to a place that will honor heaven
and set you on a rock.
You're important in My kingdom.
Think about this–and hold fast
to your calling.
Don't let go.

Don't allow yourselves to be weary
or disheartened in planting good seeds,
for the season of reaping the wonderful harvest
you've planted is coming!

GALATIANS 6:9 TPT

May 11

I encourage you today to tap into My Spirit within you
and be reassured.
You have great power within you.
You were created to look to Me,
and not to the world or yourself, for power or gratification.
Philosophy won't honor you. Exercise and diet can't feed
your spirit without My Spirit.
Your brothers and sisters can't give you what I give you.
Even those you work with and work for
can't value you as I do.
Honor and esteem are heavenly merits, bestowed by Me.
I see your work and I know your heart.
Come to Me, dear one. I'm your audience of one,
who grants approval with the accumulated voice of eternity.

You can make many plans,
but the LORD's purpose will prevail.

PROVERBS 19:21 NLT

May 12

Let go of the superstition and false assumption
that losing and misplacing things is a natural,
normal phenomenon. Losses of this sort
are not natural and normal
when you, and everything you possess, belong to Me.
There is no misplacing things in the kingdom of heaven.
Proclaim today that you'll stop
losing and misplacing things in your house,
in your pocket, in your car,
when you travel, when you stay put–
at all times and everywhere in your life because
I don't want anything to rout or intrude
on your time, energy, and peace.
I want you alert and aware with My mind.
Possess the glory of God in your life,
for this is normal and natural.
I'm a God of abundance, and I want you
to hold on to what's yours.

In your lives you must think and act like Christ Jesus.
Christ himself was like God in everything. But he
did not think that being equal with God was something
to be used for his own benefit.

PHILIPPIANS 2:5-6 NCV

May 13

I hear your questions. I'm here to answer you.
I've told you in My Word
to ask because I want you to receive.
The questions that stir in your heart
and in your mind are in My heart and mind
to answer you. You have My Spirit of truth
and wisdom in you, and you have My mind.
I fulfill all of your needs, and I answer
all your questions. Sometimes the answers
aren't what you want to hear, and sometimes
the answers are far off. But notice, My child,
I don't withhold wisdom from you.
Ask Me for wisdom and understanding,
and you'll be filled.

I will answer your cry for help every time you pray,
and you will find and feel my presence
even in your time of pressure and trouble.
I will be your glorious hero and give you a feast.

PSALM 91:15 TPT

May 14

Not everything
that you consider a need
is a need,
but more of a want,
a desire,
or even a curiosity.
You want good things,
and you want to be free
of suffering.
I want the same for you,
dear one.
All needs are fulfilled
in your love for Me.

"You shall love the Lord your God with all your heart,
and with all your soul, and with all your might."

Deuteronomy 6:5 nrsv

May 15

My ways are beyond understanding.
Yet you wonder and you fuss in your heart,
and ask Me why. I'll answer your whys
because I love you. I don't do harm,
nor do I do damage on earth. I'm not the destroyer.
Don't attribute the works of the devil to Me.
The trouble with asking Me why is that you want
an immediate answer. The answers come to you,
My child, in different ways. Often times
the answers come to you in unexpected ways.
Carry the question "why" into the back porch
of your heart and let it remain there.
Now is the hour of trust.
All will become clear in time,
and the front door to understanding
will open wide for you.
The Lord grants wisdom!
From his mouth come knowledge and understanding.
He grants a treasure of common sense to the honest.
He is a shield to those who walk with integrity.

The Lord grants wisdom!
From his mouth come knowledge and understanding.
He grants a treasure of common sense to the honest.
He is a shield to those who walk with integrity.

Proverbs 2:6-7 NLT

May 16

Today's a good day to rest
from your emotions.
Breathe and let go.
Think on your blessings
and the good things I've brought to your life.
Be at peace, for all is good.
I have everything concerning you
perfectly ordered
and under control.

Let the peace of Christ rule in your hearts,
since as members of one body you were called to peace.
And be thankful.

COLOSSIANS 3:15 NIV

May 17

You may feel bad
when you see someone doing
what you wish you could do,
but, dear child, I have work for you
that only you can do and nobody else.
The work and the life of other people
is theirs to manage and to be responsible for.
I want you to be grateful for the gifts
I've given you, which are many,
and I want you to multiply them.
I don't want you to look at those of others,
but only look
at what I've called you to do.
Focus on yourself today.
All day.

Isn't it obvious that all runners on the racetrack keep on running
to win, but only one receives the victor's prize?
Yet each one of you must run the race to be victorious.

1 CORINTHIANS 9:24 TPT

May 18

I've given you many gifts,
and you have many gifts in you
to give away.
Don't withhold giving anything away.
I'll give you far more than you give away.
When I ask you to give something,
it's because I want you blessed
as well as the other person.
Increase your giving, so I can increase you
to give even more. Never hold back giving.
Today is a great opportunity for you
to look for someone in need.

The LORD God is our sun and shield.
He gives us grace and glory.
The LORD will withhold no good thing
from those who do what is right.

PSALM 84:11 NLT

May 19

Think of today as offering day.
What do you have to offer Me today?
How much is in you
that you're willing to give up for Me?
I gave you everything in abundance;
what do you give up for Me?
Perhaps it's a habit, or a way of thinking,
that's off-kilter that you could
give up for Me so that you're free
to receive more from Me.
I have so many gifts in store for you.
I'm looking forward
to what your offering will be.

Walk in the way of love, just as Christ loved us
and gave himself up for us as a fragrant offering
and sacrifice to God.

EPHESIANS 5:2 NIV

May 20

I've given you eyes to see
far more than the natural eye can see.
I created your eyes to see
into the heart of things.
You'll have opportunities today
to see beyond what the natural eye sees.
Go there. Don't be afraid
of what you might see or learn,
because it's for your good
and My glory that I give you
the rare and precious gift of sight.

The precepts of the Lord are right,
rejoicing the heart;
the commandment of the Lord is pure,
enlightening the eyes.

Psalm 19:8 esv

May 21

Your eyes are meant to see beyond
the natural. Your eyes are meant to see
into the heart and purpose of the matter.
I've blessed your eyes for seeing
as I've blessed your hands for doing.
Your eyes are meant for more than mere
looking in the natural world.
Your eyes are meant to see into My kingdom
and My ways.
Look for Me at work around you.
Look for Me in those you meet
as well as those in your circle of influence.
I'm drawing you further into spiritual vision.
Today is a day of opportunity.

Help me turn my eyes away from illusions
so that I pursue only that which is true;
drench my soul with life as I walk in your paths.

PSALM 119:37 TPT

May 22

Expect blessings
to come your way today
from unexpected places.
When you pray
and ask Me to move
in every area of your life
and in the lives of others,
I'll respond with answers
you don't expect,
but sometimes
not as soon as you'd like.
Observe today as you encounter
new challenges,
the unexpected answers and blessings
coming your way.

The blessing of the LORD makes a person rich,
and he adds no sorrow with it.

PROVERBS 10:22 NLT

May 23

Every hour you live is an anthem
and praise to the life-changing work
that I'm doing in you.
There's nothing
about you that's unimportant.
Let your mind be steeped
in My mind hour after hour,
all day and night.
All the visible world
is sustained by the invisible,
so all your trials are little parades
in the grand procession of My heroes.
Be heroic today.

By Him all things were created that are in heaven
and that are on earth, visible and invisible,
whether thrones or dominions or principalities or powers.
All things were created through Him and for Him.

COLOSSIANS 1:16 NKJV

May 24

When you look at Me,
you can see yourself more clearly.
Recognize yourself in My mirror.
Listen to what you talk about with an attentive ear.
Realize those whom you love are more precious
than you imagined.
Staring at your reflection
in the light of My image,
you can now see
what you've ignored or left undone.
You can see what's missing,
and decide to make changes
to be the blessing you were called to be.

God created man in His own image;
in the image of God He created him;
male and female He created them.

GENESIS 1:27 NKJV

May 25

This day is sacred.
You're part of the character of heaven;
you're not a bystander,
nor are you a mere interested observer.
You're a bringer of life.
Think of everything you do
as holy unto Me.
The simplest of tasks
are holy in My eyes.
Whether you work in the kitchen,
garage, operating room, courtroom,
classroom, or home, all is important to Me.
Hold this day up to Me as sacred.

This is the very day of the Lord that brings gladness and joy,
filling our hearts with glee.

Psalm 118:24 TPT

May 26

You were born to move mountains,
and mountains aren't always easy
to move. Some mountains are meant
to climb and others are meant to move.
Still others are meant to stand near and listen to.
It was at Mount Sinai that the children of Israel
fled from Me in terror when the thundering
and lightning and shaking of My presence
came down to them. Only Moses stayed
near the mountain rejoicing and delighting
in the horrifying turmoil of the living manifestation
of My presence. Sometimes the mountain you face
is a place to test how much of My power
you're able to recognize and handle.
How close can you come to Me?

"You speak to us, and we will listen;
but do not let God speak to us, lest we die."

EXODUS 20:19 ESV

May 27

If you're going to move the mountains
that loom up on the highway of your life,
and if you're going to shove aside the detours
that block your path, get ready.
In order to move the mountain, you must first meet
the challenge of the mountain
because the foot of the mountain is barbed with lies
and subtle temptations meant to discourage you
from continuing your journey.
You'll meet the bad weather of false friendships;
you'll tread the briar patches of lack of money,
and the rocky terrain of misplaced affections, lost jobs,
family hassles, and even poor health.
Draw close to Me, breathe in
the power of My name, and then with
the undefeatable mountain-moving machinery
of prayer, and with a simple whisper of faith,
you'll move the mountain. As easy as that.

Be of sober spirit, be on the alert.
Your adversary, the devil, prowls around like a roaring lion,
seeking someone to devour.

1 PETER 5:8 NASB

May 28

Sit quietly with Me and listen.
Ask for nothing and say nothing.
Just sit quietly with Me.
It may be difficult to do at first,
but as you concentrate on simply sitting with Me,
you'll begin to relax and you'll sense My presence
in the stillness.
It's here your soul can be energized
as you become more alert
to My voice and My presence.
I want to help you make the choices
you must make today.
Recognize My voice in the quiet of your heart.

I don't depend on my own strength to accomplish this;
however I do have one compelling focus:
I forget all of the past as I fasten my heart to the future instead.
I run straight for the divine invitation of reaching the heavenly goal
and gaining the victory-prize through the anointing of Jesus.

PHILIPPIANS 3:13-14 TPT

May 29

Observe the competing interests
around you and be the voice
of reason and justice.
Let your heart beat
for the well-being of others.
Bring your personal influence   .
into the world around you
with love. In everything you do
and say, know that you are called
to a higher walk,
and your shield of faith
will not allow the growling mouths
of strife and ambition
to sink their teeth into you.

Owe nothing to anyone—
except for your obligation to love one another.
If you love your neighbor,
you will fulfill the requirements of God's law.

ROMANS 13:8 NLT

May 30

Expect the unexpected today.
Be aware that you're moving
in a new direction,
and I'm with you every step of the way.
Don't be afraid to require more strength
of your body today.
I'm your healer, your strength,
and your deliverer.
Don't be afraid to step out
where you've never stepped before.
I'm going ahead of you
and preparing everything.

**Whether you turn to the right or to the left,
your ears will hear a voice behind you, saying,
"This is the way; walk in it."**

ISAIAH 30:21 NIV

May 31

Your heart is My garden, dear one,
and I'm inside your heart along with
today's many issues and concerns churning about.
I reach over as your loving divine gardener and whisper,
"Peace, be still," and lo and behold,
things quiet down. Where I am,
the atmosphere of heaven pervades,
so I want you to imagine the beauty and tranquil joys
of heaven permeating your heart right now.
Think about the wonderful
surprises of heaven's nature to discover
at this moment living in your heart,
where I'm a permanent resident.
Come, tend your garden today
with the sweet, nourishing love that's in you.

I have entered my garden, my treasure, my bride!
I gather myrrh with my spices
and eat honeycomb with my honey.
I drink wine with my milk.

SONG OF SONGS 5:1 NLT

JUNE

"Indeed the Kingdom of God

is within you."

LUKE 17:21 NKJV

June 1

As the earth blossoms,
expect My Spirit to create havoc
with those powers that have detoured
My purposes in your life.
Expect much fruit in this hour.
But you must know who you are in Me!
Learn to be accustomed to standing strong.
The months of favor ahead
are like a garden of royal testing.
How will you manage favor?
How will you manage an outpouring
of My Spirit?
I say walk by faith, not by sight.
Take this word seriously
and act with your whole being.
My chosen one,
I've pressed the call button for you.

He will be standing firm like a flourishing tree planted by God's design,
deeply rooted by the brooks of bliss, bearing fruit in every season of his
life. He is never dry, never fainting, ever blessed, ever prosperous.

ISAIAH 58:11 TPT

June 2

I'm walking with you
in the glory of goodness and mercy
that follows you every day of your life.
Won't you take time
to pause and worship your God?
I know you are busy,
but I didn't call you to be busy.
I called you to be about My purposes.
Never forget, if there's a burden
to carry, choose the light one
and don't let your heart
be troubled with busyness.
Allow yourself to stop
and rest a while with Me today.
Everything will be completed
right on time.

"Take my yoke upon you and learn from me,
for I am gentle and humble in heart,
and you will find rest for your souls."

MATTHEW 11:29 NIV

June 3

Walk in the power that lives in you.
I speak to your heart
by My Spirit, and I'm leading
you by your hand.
Hold on to My hand tightly.
Don't let go.
I never yank or pull you; no–
I gently lead you.
Open your ears and be blessed
with words of life
that I breathe into your soul.
I have so much to tell you
as we walk together, and I love
to hear your voice as we walk.
In all the world there's no greater walk
than the one you walk with Me.
Our fellowship is the sweetest fellowship
on earth. Cherish this moment.

**"I will also walk among you and be your God,
and you shall be My people."**

LEVITICUS 26:12 NASB

June 4

A shift of events is about to occur
and you're going to experience
a release of My favor
in those areas
you've been praying about.
When I release favor on you,
the world around you
is favored because I've called you
to be a blessing to the world.
Release what I give you
without restraint
and permit yourself
to give to others what you receive.

"How satisfied you are when you demonstrate tender mercy!
For tender mercy will be demonstrated to you."

MATTHEW 5:7 TPT

June 5

Expect favor
in your personal relationships.
I want to bring healing
to relationships
that the devil has poisoned.
Pray and I'll return the darts
of the evil one to his abode.
You haven't fought against
flesh and blood, but against powers
and principalities beyond human control.
I see everything, and I'm returning
every divisive curse to their source
to see you, My beloved,
free to love and be loved.

We do not wrestle against flesh and blood, but against principalities,
against powers, against the rulers of the darkness of this age,
against spiritual hosts of wickedness in the heavenly places.

EPHESIANS 6:12 NKJV

June 6

Keep on anticipating My hand
to accomplish great things
in your midst because of your prayers.
Many of My children aren't prepared
for what I'm accomplishing
in the world by My Spirit,
but many are praying, and
My hand isn't shortened
that I can't respond and save.
I'm combing every corner of the earth
observing those I can trust.
Be wise in this hour. Be wise.
It's a time to climb into
the secret place of the Most High
and spend much more time in My presence
because My eyes are going to and fro
across the entire globe looking for a heart
like yours.

The eyes of the LORD search the whole earth in order to strengthen
those whose hearts are fully committed to him.

2 CHRONICLES 16:9 NLT

June 7

It's time to look deeply
into the events of your life
and not take for granted
the blessings that surround you
because I'm showing you
more than what the natural eye
can see. Today, when you receive
good news, receive it
with gladness,
for it has eternal value
and I want you to see
My purposes hidden inside
every blessing.

"You will know the truth,
and the truth will set you free."

JOHN 8:32 NLT

June 8

Don't forget to pause and thank Me
for the many blessings
you receive. If you trip and fall,
My angels are there to catch you.
When you slip on the tail of deceit and disharmony,
I'm there to pull you up and set you back
on your path.
New challenges are heading your way
and your life will be blessed exponentially
as you meet these challenges
with the power and wisdom of My Spirit.
You have the inner resources
to tackle all challenges and come out
victorious in every case. Receive
My renewed blessing and energy,
and know that your walk is anointed,
for I have gone before you.

That's where he restores and revives my life. He opens before me
pathways to God's pleasure and leads me along in his footsteps of
righteousness so that I can bring honor to his name.

PSALM 23:3 TPT

June 9

You ask Me for a miracle, and
I have a miracle for you today.
Believe that you've received
what you've asked for.
I performed hundreds of miracles
for the Israelites and yet they rebelled
and constantly lost heart.
I parted the Red Sea, dropped manna down
from heaven as food, led My people
to the Promised Land,
and in spite of miracle upon miracle,
they defied Me.
Miracles aren't the food that feeds the
soul. If you love Me, love Me more
than the miracles.

Israel saw the great power that the LORD used against the Egyptians,
so the people feared the LORD, and they believed in the LORD
and in his servant Moses.

EXODUS 14:31 ESV

June 10

Today, My children continually ask Me
for miracles, and I answer because
I love to perform miracles enforcing
the fulfillment of My purposes and My will.
I want My will to be done on earth
as in heaven. Nothing can stop My will
from being accomplished. Nothing can still
My voice. Nothing can silence My Spirit.
I'm not a parlor-game god, and I'm not
a talented cosmic magician performing tricks
to tantalize a human audience.
I am the creator of heaven and earth.
When you ask Me for a miracle,
look for My will within the miracle,
and it'll be done.
Miracles are born out of the abundance of faith.

"Anyone who believes in me will do the same works I have done,
and even greater works, because I am going to be with the Father."

JOHN 14:12 NLT

June 11

My child, love is built on faith,
and it's faith that moves mountains.
Moving a mountain into the sea
serves no redemptive purpose in itself.
It can be accomplished without Me
with trucks and cranes and modern
machinery. Bodies are healed every day
without My intervention through
medical treatment. Yet I tell you, faith the size
of a mustard seed is sufficient to proclaim
earth-moving miracles. The time is coming
when the only way to move insurmountable
trials out of your way is through
the authority and power of your faith.
Prepare for that day.

Your life and ministry must not be disgraced,
for you are to be a pure container of Christ
and dedicated to the honorable purposes of your Master,
prepared for every good work that he gives you to do.

2 TIMOTHY 2:21 TPT

June 12

You're called and chosen by Me.
I hold you in the palm of My hand.
Nothing and nobody can take you
out of My hand. When I walked
the earth, I spoke life-empowered words
that birthed miracles, healed, and changed lives,
and I haven't changed. I'm the same
yesterday, today, and forever.
Face this day without apology.
Be confident in who you are,
chosen and beloved.

I pray with great faith for you, because I'm fully convinced
that the One who began this glorious work in you
will faithfully continue the process of maturing you
and will put his finishing touches to it
until the unveiling of our Lord Jesus Christ!

PHILIPPIANS 1:6 TPT

June 13

I invite you to walk yoked with Me today.
If you look at two oxen yoked together
they must walk at the exact same pace
to get anywhere.
When you're yoked to Me, your pace
must be the same as Mine. And yoked
together, we carry the same light burden.
Remember, My burden is light.
Yoked with Me, you'll walk at a peaceful,
happy pace with a light, easy burden,
the very same as Mine. If you drag your feet,
try to run ahead of Me, or yank to one
direction or another, the yoke will grieve
your neck. Which do you choose today?

"My yoke is easy and my burden is light."

MATTHEW 11:30 NIV

June 14

Picture yourself walking with Me now.
Picture yourself holding My hand
and calmly walking along the path of life
with Me. I have said to come to Me
when you feel heavy burdened and I'll
give you rest. I said to yoke yourself
with Me and learn from Me because
I'm free of all cares, and My heart is humble.
This is a peaceful walk, My child, and here
with My hand in yours,
picture yourself beginning to feel
a wondrous sense of peace
enter your soul.

Be imitators of God, as beloved children;
and walk in love, just as Christ also loved you
and gave Himself up for us, an offering
and a sacrifice to God as a fragrant aroma.

EPHESIANS 5:1-2 NASB

June 15

I do everything properly and orderly
with compassion and patience.
I'm not the author of confusion,
so be careful of finding fault
with your brothers and sisters.
Be encouraging, kindhearted, and loving
even at times when you disagree,
or when things aren't being done the way
you'd like to see them done.
Remain open-minded, lighthearted
and non-judgmental.
Show mercy.
This is My will, darling child.
Be kind.

God is not a God of disorder but of peace,
as in all the meetings of God's holy people.
But be sure that everything is done properly and in order.

1 CORINTHIANS 14:33, 40 NLT

June 16

Trust My will for your work.
I'm giving you the strength and wisdom
for everything you have to accomplish
this month and this year.
I'll never ask you to do something
that you aren't able to do by the power
of My Spirit who empowers and instructs you
daily, hour-by-hour. It's important to meditate
on My Word for clarity and guidance.
Believe that I'm working in you
to make My power known in all that you do.
I'll make My power known
in your life and your work.

I will instruct you and teach you in the way you should go;
I will counsel you with my loving eye on you.

Psalm 32:8 niv

June 17

I searched for you when you were lost,
and I comforted you when you were hurt.
I rescued you, a lost orphan in the world,
and brought you into My family.
I bought your freedom with My blood;
I forgave all your sins
and created a new heart in you.
Now you can ask Me to make you wise
concerning spiritual things and I'll answer,
showing you My ways so that you'll
keep going, always full of wonder
and always thankful.
Fill your day today with humility and joy.
Others will see it and be touched.

May you be made strong with all the strength that comes from his
glorious power, and may you be prepared to endure everything with
patience, while joyfully giving thanks to the Father, who has enabled
you to share in the inheritance of the saints in the light.

COLOSSIANS 1:11-12 NRSV

June 18

Today, walk resolutely in the sweet aroma
of My Spirit
so the devil can't drag you
into the foul stink of carnality,
which may look sweetly tempting,
but look a little closer
and you'll recognize the very pit
you were pulled from.
Keep yourself from yesterday's sin.
Choose beautiful and clean today in Me
as the new you.

Give yourselves completely to God.
Stand against the devil,
and the devil will run from you.

JAMES 4:7 NCV

June 19

Think of yourself as lighting up
the atmosphere and bringing My glory
into every situation of this day.
In Me there's no darkness at all.
I am all light.
You, My darling child, are alive
on the earth to live and breathe
inside My illuminated presence
in everything
you do.

"Your lives light up the world.
Let others see your light from a distance,
for how can you hide a city that stands on a hilltop?"

MATTHEW 5:14 TPT

June 20

Nothing can keep you
from your camaraderie
with Me. Pay no attention
to the negative influences
of the world. The way to put an end
to darkness is to flip on the light.
Whenever you're overwhelmed
by tempting thoughts, come to Me immediately
and leap into the brightness of love and truth.
Let the sunshine of heavenly thoughts
paint the walls of your heart with light,
and My peace which surpasses all comprehension
will remove the shadows of worry in your mind.

I am convinced that neither death nor life, neither angels nor demons,
neither the present nor the future, nor any powers, neither height nor
depth, nor anything else in all creation, will be able to separate us from
the love of God that is in Christ Jesus our Lord.

ROMANS 8:38-39 NIV

June 21

Where's your treasure today?
Material treasures are amassed
and stored up on earth, and they
fall apart. I understand your concern
for security, but everything you possess
will eventually corrode. The nest egg you trust in
can vanish in the blink of an eye.
I have wealth for you beyond the reach of storms,
thieves, mildew, and recession. No one can serve
the master of money and Me as master of life
at the same time. It doesn't work.
Love Me and focus on the riches I offer your soul,
which are far more spectacular than material belongings.
But here's My promise to you:
I'll prosper you physically in every way
as you do the spiritual work to prosper your soul.

Those who trust in riches will be ruined,
but a good person will be healthy like a green leaf.

PROVERBS 11:28 NRSV

June 22

Don't worry about things.
Look at the birds outside your window.
They're cared for and fed by Me.
Aren't you more valuable than they?
Worrying won't add a single minute to your day.
I tell you, be clever, be smart.
Who do you think designed the clothes
worn by the lilies of the field?
It is I, with more color and creative design
than King Solomon ever imagined
in all his kingly glory.
Happiness creates beauty, dear child.
Let your happy mind take over
and let your creativity flow. Flowers and birds
are here today and gone tomorrow,
but you're in My heart forever.

"Look at the birds of the air; they do not sow or reap
or store away in barns, and yet your heavenly Father feeds them.
Are you not much more valuable than they?
Can any one of you by worrying add a single hour to your life?"

MATTHEW 6:26-27 NIV

June 23

Seek the treasures of heaven
as your true wealth.
Money has no soul or personality.
You're the one with soul and
personality. You're designed to bring
heaven to earth with all its riches.
You're My treasure as I'm your treasure.
I've placed you into the light
as a beacon to the world around you,
and you have inside you more beauty
and power than all the gold in the earth.
Trust Me in you.

"Do not store up for yourselves treasures on earth, where moths and
vermin destroy, and where thieves break in and steal. But store up
for yourselves treasures in heaven, where moths and vermin do not
destroy, and where thieves do not break in and steal."

Matthew 6:19-20 niv

June 24

Count the hurts that you've experienced
as part of the soul wealth stored up
in your heavenly bank account.
I've seen how you've suffered and yet
stood strong in Me. I've seen
how your heart has ached and how the tears
flew in torrents down your dear face.
Be lifted up today by My Holy Spirit
and encouraged. You're a bright light
to many and a comfort to those
who are going through the same valley of tears.

Love empowers us to fulfill the law of the Anointed One
as we carry each other's troubles.

GALATIANS 6:2 TPT

June 25

You're My chosen one. You're valued
and honored. I've called you out of darkness
and pulled your feet out of the mud
of life. Lift up your head today and run
from anything that tries to pull you back down.
You're not of the world. You've been born again
in My Spirit! You're in the world but you're not
a part of the world. Give up all longing to belong
to that which isn't for you. No devil has the right
to harass, hurt, or steal from you. Don't give the devil
that privilege. Demons need your permission
to hurt you. They make something appear to be good,
like a trap set for a dumb animal. Run, I say, run!

He stooped down to lift me out of danger
from the desolate pit I was in,
out of the muddy mess I had fallen into.
Now he's lifted me up into a firm, secure place
and steadied me while I walk along his ascending path.

PSALM 40:2 TPT

June 26

I'm the God of signs and wonders.
I don't change.
The miracles I performed
while I was on the earth
are common knowledge now.
I gave the same power and
authority to My apostles in the early church,
and I loved moving on the earth,
following the testimonies of those early servants
by My Holy Spirit with miracles, signs, and wonders,
the same as today. I assign special holy gifts
to each of My children.
I want you to function in your special gifts today.

"People of Israel, listen to the facts. Jesus, the Victorious,
was a Man on a divine mission whose authority was clearly proven.
For you know how God performed many powerful miracles,
signs, and wonders through him."

ACTS 2:22 TPT

June 27

When you ask, believe
that you've received your answers.
Have My mind deeply embedded
in your mind. Connect with Me now.
You have all the strength
and energy you need to accomplish
what you're to do today
because you're empowered
by Me every single day.
I'll always answer you when you pray.
When you and I are one, we want the same things.
And when I want a thing done, it'll be done.
That's a promise.

For this I toil and struggle with all the energy
that he powerfully inspires within me.

COLOSSIANS 1:29 NRSV

June 28

Don't allow yourself to think
gloomy, depressing thoughts
when I've given you a new mind.
It's with your renewed mind
that you can understand everything
I tell you, and it's with
your renewed mind
that confusion is banished.
Without Me the world is disoriented
and churning on broken wheels.
You, however, are beautifully transformed
by the renewing of your mind,
and equipped to prove to yourself
and the world My good and perfect will.

God designed us to feel remorse over sin in order to produce
repentance that leads to victory. This leaves us with no regrets.
But the sorrow of the world works death.

2 Corinthians 7:10 tpt

June 29

Be brave today, and take a chance.
Step out into the unknown.
Trust Me. I'm here to help you
and encourage you.
Feel yourself complete in Me.
Sense My presence with you
throughout this day and night.
I'm here to rescue you from bad thinking
and bad choices.
I won't let you fall.

**The Lord will be your confidence
and will keep your foot from being caught.**

Proverbs 3:26 esv

June 30

Focus. Breathe in a deep breath
and focus your thoughts
on this: All is well.
I'm on My throne
and there's nothing to be flustered about.
I'm the source of everything you need.
You're so eager to do something for Me,
but I'm asking you to pause and focus
on being at peace. Often My children
busy themselves at tasks I don't require.
It's not you who decides
what needs to be done for Me
and My kingdom.
I make that call.

**Don't lose your bold, courageous faith,
for you are destined for a great reward!**
Hebrews 10:35 tpt

JULY

Delight yourself also in the LORD,

And He shall give you

the desires of your heart.

PSALM 37:4 NKJV

July 1

Beware of spending more time
doing things for Me
than you spend being with Me.
Much work done for Me in My name
is not initiated by Me.
Everything man can do for Me
I can do without man's help.
Here is what I want:
I want you to be fully transformed
and renewed by My Holy Spirit.
This, darling child, is the work I choose for you.

"You must remain in life-union with me, for I remain in life-union with you. For as a branch severed from the vine will not bear fruit, so your life will be fruitless unless you live your life intimately joined to mine."

John 15:4 TPT

July 2

Present yourself, wholly to Me,
body, soul, and spirit
as a living sacrifice,
which is the reasonable behavior
of a loyal disciple. Are you any different
from My early disciples
who preached the Gospel
to the ancient world?
I want you to walk a holy walk
with Me so charged with faith and joy
that your modern world is stunned
into awakening.

I urge you, brothers and sisters, in view of God's mercy, to offer your
bodies as a living sacrifice, holy and pleasing to God—this is your true
and proper worship. Do not conform to the pattern of this world, but
be transformed by the renewing of your mind.

ROMANS 12:1-2 NIV

July 3

I'm preparing you to stand strong
in the face of trouble
and adversity. Be bold. Be strong.
Be resolute.
Don't look to the left or to the right
for your help. I'm right here
beside you and in you.
Adore Me and allow yourself
to sink into the warmth of forgiveness.
I took your shame and your fear.
You're now free to be all
that I've called you to be
from the beginning.

Do not fear, for I am with you; do not be dismayed,
for I am your God. I will strengthen you and help you;
I will uphold you with my righteous right hand.

Isaiah 41:10 NIV

July 4

The clamor of your busy plans
can snuff out or distort the whisper
of My still, small voice.
I want you
to walk faithful in all your ways,
loyal to Me in sweet adoration.
Be drawn to study My Word
and lift up praises to Me.
Come to Me today in quiet adoration.
I have much to share with you.

Their wisdom will guide you wherever you go and keep you from
bringing harm to yourself. Their instruction will whisper to you at
every sunrise and direct you through a brand-new day. For truth is a
bright beam of light shining into every area of your life, instructing and
correcting you to discover the ways to godly living.

PROVERBS 6:22-23 TPT

July 5

My forgiveness is forever.
You won't go back to the way things were.
I delivered you from the past
in one lightning blast of forgiveness,
and no shame or dishonor can come near you,
for in the sight of heaven you're clean,
loved, and beautiful. Only I can make all things new
and create a brand new heart in a person
No philosophy or positive thought can create all things new.
I am God, and to Me you're worth
dying for. I did it for you.

You kissed my heart with forgiveness, in spite of all I've done.
You've healed me inside and out from every disease.
You've rescued me from hell and saved my life.
You've crowned me with love and mercy.

PSALM 103:3-4 TPT

July 6

Take your power today and be confident
that I've begun a new thing in you.
You're standing on a solid rock. You're not
stuck in sludge. Hold on to Me.
Tell yourself the truth.
I'm getting rid of the remnants of yesterday's
unfortunate choices. I'm washing the memories
of all ungodliness from your mind.
Don't let the devil torment you by rehashing the past because
there's no condemnation toward you
for anything whatsoever. My blood has covered
every sin, and you are forgiven completely.
You've found your forever freedom with Me.

"I will cleanse them from all their iniquity by which they have sinned
against Me, and I will pardon all their iniquities by which they have
sinned and by which they have transgressed against Me."

JEREMIAH 33:8 NKJV

July 7

I was there before the world began,
so you can depend on Me for your needs today.
I know the thoughts of humans
and I know the ways of the world better than you.
Let go of your anxious, tight grip on all your plans
and concerns, and give them to Me.
Place the pressures and responsibilities
in My capable hands. I'm using
everything in your life to create something good.
My Holy Spirit is breathing the heart and mind
of God into your spirit today.
Fall in love with My words and hear My voice
calling you to be holy as I am holy,
because everything concerning you is kissed with favor.
It's holiness you are really seeking.

This is why we abandon everything morally impure and all forms of
wicked conduct. Instead, with a sensitive spirit we absorb God's Word,
which has been implanted within our nature, for the Word of Life has
power to continually deliver us.

JAMES 1:21 TPT

July 8

You're easy to love, dear one,
and because you're so easy to love,
make it easy for yourself to love others.
All you have to do is see Me
in the eyes and lives of other people.
This is a commandment to own.
I've said that the person who keeps
My commandments is one who loves Me,
and the chief commandment I gave you
is to love one another.

"A new commandment I give to you, that you love one another;
as I have loved you, that you also love one another."

JOHN 13:34 NKJV

July 9

Develop a listening ear
so that My Spirit can speak to you
anywhere about anything.
Keep My Word humming
in your heart, and keep your vision
of Me ever before you.
Many good things lie ahead for you today!

I have hidden your word in my heart
that I might not sin against you.

PSALM 119:11 NIV

July 10

Knowledge is important,
but human knowledge can clutter
the atmosphere with empty prattle.
Human knowledge reflects reality,
but cannot fully engage in the eternal
substance of reality.
Human knowledge of Me is perfunctory and vain.
I'm far greater, mightier, wiser than
what the worldly mind knows of Me.
When you're looking for knowledge,
you're looking for Me!

**Anyone who claims to know something
does not yet have the necessary knowledge;**

1 CORINTHIANS 8:2 NRSV

July 11

There's a definite difference
between spending your time
seeking answers to your questions
and seeking Me.
When you're one with Me,
I'll open to you the answers
you seek.
Today is a day
of answered questions for you.

"Call to me and I will answer you,
and will tell you great and hidden things
that you have not known."

JEREMIAH 33:3 ESV

July 12

To be holy means to be set apart
from the mundane and the hopeless.
To be holy means to be luminous with joy;
it means to willingly walk away
from the sins that once held you trapped.
Holiness is a clean and untarnished condition.
Come to heaven's laundry to get
your daily cleanse for walking
your holy walk with your head held high.
Let the happiness inside you leap from you
like magnets drawing others to Me.

Because we have these promises, dear friends, let us cleanse ourselves
from everything that can defile our body or spirit. And let us work
toward complete holiness because we fear God.

2 CORINTHIANS 7:1 NLT

July 13

True holiness is found in My presence.
You may do many things
that are religious in nature
but true holiness is not religious;
holiness is an attitude of purity
and a compassionate, loving way of life
led by My Holy Spirit.
The Pharisees were religious;
they were set apart, but they
weren't led by My Spirit.
Proud and self-righteous, they were
without heart and capable of murder.
I want you to be motivated by compassion
and by My love. I gave My life
so you could know how to love.

"But I warn you—unless your righteousness is better than the righteousness of the teachers of religious law and the Pharisees, you will never enter the Kingdom of Heaven!"

MATTHEW 5:20 NLT

July 14

I speak to your heart
and My voice
is an inner voice.
You'll receive confirmations
of what you hear from Me today.
Open your Bible to the book of John
for My Words
to take flight in your soul.
Allow what I'm telling you
to penetrate into your day
because what you do next will shift
your life in a new direction.

**In the beginning was the Word,
and the Word was with God,
and the Word was God.**

JOHN 1:1 NIV

July 15

If you're puzzled and disturbed
at the paradoxes of life,
take some time to look at yourself
in the light of the world around you
and within you.
Can you be at peace and rest
in the disquieted moments of unknowing?
Can you allow yourself to honor the mysteries
of an inconsistent world, rather than to fret and fear?
There's much wisdom to be had for you today
in the holy space of waiting, watching, and praying.

Trust in the Lord completely,
and do not rely on your own opinions.
With all your heart rely on him to guide you,
and he will lead you in every decision you make.
Become intimate with him in whatever you do,
and he will lead you wherever you go.

PROVERBS 3:5-6 TPT

July 16

I'm granting your spirit right now, this moment,
new empowering strength,
according to all of My riches in glory.
You need supernatural strength today
which can only be had through My Spirit.
Lay down all doubts and flimsy arguments,
and let Me burst forth alive and vibrant in your heart,
so you'll be solidly rooted and grounded
in who you are in Me.
I know you, dear one, and I love
filling you with the fullness of My love.

I pray that Christ will live in your hearts by faith and that your life will be strong in love and be built on love. And I pray that you and all God's holy people will have the power to understand the greatness of Christ's love— how wide and how long and how high and how deep that love is. Christ's love is greater than anyone can ever know, but I pray that you will be able to know that love. Then you can be filled with the fullness of God.

Ephesians 3:17-19 ncv

July 17

Be happy
you have a tender conscience.
A tender conscience is what made
My servant, David, great.
It wasn't a perfect life,
but his tender conscience
that made him a man
after My own heart.
I understand you.
I understand everything.
I love your tender heart.
I'm ever walking beside you,
so enjoy this day and be happy
in the fullness of who you are.

After removing him, God raised up David to be king, for God said of
him, "I have found in David, son of Jesse, a man who always pursues
my heart and will accomplish all that I have destined him to do."

ACTS 13:22 TPT

July 18

Be aware of the words
you tell yourself.
Don't be swift to ingest words
into your spirit
that aren't of Me.
Turn a deaf ear
to discouraging words
born in the root of a curse.
I lift you up
and out of the tangle
of worldly, carnal jabber,
even when the curse comes from
yourself.
Listen for and speak
the truth only.

"I will watch my ways and keep my tongue from sin;
I will put a muzzle on my mouth while in the presence of the wicked."
So I remained utterly silent, not even saying anything good.
But my anguish increased.

PSALM 39:1-2 NIV

July 19

It's better to stay quiet
and keep your tongue
from speaking
than to eat the bitter fruit
of regret later on.
It's better to be silent
than to say something
today that you'll
thump your head for tomorrow.
You're the master
of your unspoken words.
Guard your tongue well today.

**Those who are careful about what they say
keep themselves out of trouble.**

PROVERBS 21:23 NCV

July 20

Be aware and on your guard
so you aren't carried away
by the reckless behavior of others.
People who don't really care
about you may entice you to do
that which isn't good for you,
My beloved child, and I don't want you
to be duped by those who
twist and misconstrue My Word
to their own satisfaction and whim.
Hold on tight to the truth and the gifts
I've given you. Use your inner power
and this time to grow spiritually strong,
for you are well able.

Be on your guard so that you are not carried away by the error of
unprincipled men and fall from your own steadfastness, but grow
in the grace and knowledge of our Lord and Savior Jesus Christ.
To Him be the glory, both now and to the day of eternity.

2 Peter 3:17-18 nasb

July 21

I'm opening doors
that have been closed;
you're going to see transformation
take place in relationships
that have previously
been distant and cool.
Favor is being drawn to you
because you've been faithful to Me.
I've been with you as you've patiently
stood strong and trusted Me.
You're going to see changes
take place in the attitude
of opposing and indifferent forces.
Be wise as you walk through
the new open doors
and don't forget to thank Me.

Let me be clear, the Anointed One has set us free—not partially, but
completely and wonderfully free! We must always cherish this truth
and stubbornly refuse to go back into the bondage of our past.

GALATIANS 5:1 TPT

July 22

I respond to your every call
for guidance and help
in handling matters
too big for you.
I am putting wisdom
into your mouth.
I'm opening your awareness
to speak from a deep place
of understanding and integrity.
Your words will flow from you
with intelligent thoughtfulness.
Tell yourself no longer
will you spurt words emotionally, without control.
All the skills you need
are within you.

My God shall supply all your need
according to His riches in glory by Christ Jesus.

PHILIPPIANS 4:19 NKJV

July 23

My child, I'll never forsake you
nor break My promises to you.
I'm faithful and loyal to you.
I'll never allow you to fall into
the cracks of oblivion and loss
because I've made a covenant,
a holy, eternal agreement with you
to bless you.
I've promised to provide your every need,
and it is so. My promises can never be broken.
You're My seed and My offspring.
All I have is yours.

Since you've been united to Jesus the Messiah, you are now Abraham's
"child" and inherit all the promises of the kingdom realm!

GALATIANS 3:29 TPT

July 24

There's no need
to fight your own battles.
When you pray, "Lord, increase my faith,"
I answer you, and then I observe with delight
as you develop deeper faith
by the power of My Holy Spirit.
I always go to battle for you.
You're never, ever without help.
I've prepared a way before you
and nothing will impede My purposes
in your life. Stay strong!
Your faith is your fierce
and powerful defender.
Let nothing take it from you.

Use the shield of faith with which you can stop
all the burning arrows of the Evil One.

EPHESIANS 6:16 NCV

July 25

When you make a mistake,
turn to Me and let Me deal
with the situation.
I'll help you reconcile what went amiss.
I'm your advocate and your defense.
Never succumb to self-recrimination
or despair. I'm the healer of all wounds.
I heal the mind, the emotions, and the body.
I forgive, mend, and repair.
The devil wants to age you
with sleeplessness,
but I'm here to rescue you.
Climb into My arms where all is good.
I love you and we'll do this together.

"Come now, and let us reason together," says the LORD,
"Though your sins are like scarlet, they shall be as white as snow;
Though they are red like crimson, they shall be as wool."

ISAIAH 1:18 NKJV

July 26

You're in command of far more
than you realize.
Align your mind
with My mind,
and take your rightful position
as My heir.
Begin to apply
more authority by speaking
and acting on My written Word.
It's faith that moves mountains,
not arguments.

Then God said, "Let us make human beings in our image, to be like us.
They will reign over the fish in the sea, the birds in the sky,
the livestock, all the wild animals on the earth,
and the small animals that scurry along the ground."

GENESIS 1:26 NLT

July 27

When anxious thoughts
crowd your mind
remember this period of time
is but a small interval
in the whole, grand picture
of your life.
My purposes are yet
to be fulfilled,
and there is much joy
and excitement ahead for you.
In My divine wisdom,
I know what's best.
I'm revealing more of Myself
to you, and you're going to see
this period of time swept into the past
where you'll be anxious no more.
Let it begin today.

In the multitude of my anxieties within me,
Your comforts delight my soul.

Psalm 94:19 NKJV

July 28

Don't accept less today.
If you feel a void inside,
know that I'm here
to show you exactly
how to fill that void.
The devil is ready and eager
to bind you with his deadly agenda,
and I'm stretching out My hand
of courage and fulfillment to you.
so you'll stand strong.
I'll always swoop you up and out
of the void to set you on a high place,
when you call out to Me
for help. I have a new
and exciting fruitful activity
planned for you–personally designed by Me!

God is my protection. He makes my way free from fault.
He makes me like a deer that does not stumble;
he helps me stand on the steep mountains.

2 SAMUEL 22:33-34 NCV

July 29

Never allow an offense to take root
in your mind, to fester and spoil
your sleep. When you love Me
and keep yourself grounded
in My Word, you'll rise up
praying strong, and you'll
brush the offenses off
like lint on a sock.
Know your place in
My kingdom and don't allow
momentary interferences
to invade your peace.
Praise Me and be content today.

I will praise you as long as I live,
and in your name I will lift up my hands.
I will be fully satisfied as with the richest of foods;
with singing lips my mouth will praise you.

PSALM 63:4-5 NIV

July 30

I'm granting you new insight
into matters you aren't aware of.
I'm enlarging your gift
of knowledge to open up
many new areas
of possibilities for you.
Never let frustration overtake you.
You're going forward
with My favor just as I've promised
you in My Word.
There'll be no defeat on your path.
Rejoice in My goodness
as I lead your faith-driven efforts
to new channels of success.
Use the gifts I've given you
and begin to thrive in abundance.

I pray that the light of God will illuminate the eyes of your imagination,
flooding you with light, until you experience the full revelation of the
hope of his calling—that is, the wealth of God's glorious inheritances
that he finds in us, his holy ones!

EPHESIANS 1:18 TPT

July 31

You're free to soar, to fly
with nothing blocking
your way. Go, I say, go!
Enjoy and be fruitful!
I'm with you today
and always as you take wing,
putting behind you
all that has disturbed you
or tried to hinder
your high calling in Me.
Your spiritual muscles
are being strengthened
as you pray and worship Me.
I'll give you energy without limit.

**He gives power to the weak
and strength to the powerless.**

Isaiah 40:29 NLT

AUGUST

Great is the LORD,

and greatly to be praised;

And His greatness is unsearchable.

PSALM 145:3 NKJV

August 1

I have many things to speak to you
about as we walk together.
I have many gifts from My holy treasury
to enhance your life and give you deeper purpose,
meaning, and understanding into your calling.
I've promised to lead, prosper, and heal you,
and My promises are eternal.
They can't be broken.
I want you to live in health
and security, and I want you
to fulfill the work I've given you to do.
Don't accept the battering lies
of the enemy to discourage you.
I'll never let you go, and you'll succeed
in everything I've given you to do.

To the one who pleases him God gives wisdom and knowledge and joy;
but to the sinner he gives the work of gathering and heaping,
only to give to one who pleases God.
This also is vanity and a chasing after wind.

ECCLESIASTES 2:26 NRSV

August 2

Don't be afraid
to come to Me
to ask Me for forgiveness.
There's a continual,
unending flow
of forgiveness and grace
in My heart,
enough to cover the world.
I am very forgiving,
and I love you
as no human
can love you.

"For this reason I say to you, her sins, which are many, have been
forgiven, for she loved much; but he who is forgiven little, loves little."
Then He said to her, "Your sins have been forgiven."

LUKE 7:47-48 NASB

August 3

I want you to receive and proclaim
the truth about who you are
and what your inheritance in Me
consists of. I gladly heal you
and grant you health and security.
It begins in your soul.
I heal the wounds of your soul
and the disturbances of your mind.
I take My holy broom
and sweep through your tangled emotions
so you can see and discern clearly.
I give you holy direction to make
heavenly choices.
I deliver you from dark,
negative thought patterns.
Today, learn about the benefits
that are yours and enjoy your life as the blessed
child of God you are.

Let all that I am praise the LORD;
may I never forget the good things he does for me.

PSALM 103:2 NLT

August 4

I've given you work to do, and a holy calling.
Enjoy My perfect will. What is My will?
My will for you is to perfect
everything concerning you.
My will is to fulfill
and complete that which I began
in you. My will is to empower
and bless you every step of your walk
with Me. My will is to see you
rise up strong in Me
with the understanding that
only that which is done through Me lasts.
My will is that you know
you're being wondrously transformed
by My mighty power,
and you're now a channel of My blessing
to the world.

I delight to fulfill your will, my God,
for your living words are written upon the pages of my heart.

PSALM 40:8 TPT

August 5

Just as I walked with Adam and Eve
in the Garden of Eden,
I walk with you.
I walk and talk with you
every day, even when you aren't aware
of Me. When you pray and ask Me
to be with you, I want you to know
I'm already with you.
My name, Immanuel, means "God with us."
I'm with you always.
What can separate you from Me?
Nothing.
When you're Mine, you're Mine.
There's no longer any separation between us.
We're united by My Spirit.
Are you ready to go for a walk with me?

"Teach these new disciples to obey
all the commands I have given you.
And be sure of this: I am with you always,
even to the end of the age."

MATTHEW 28:20 NLT

August 6

Good things were kept from you
when you were bopping around in sin,
but I forgave
and I'll go on forgiving.
I alone forgive all sin
and I alone heal.
I found you and loved you
out of the garbage bucket
of hopelessness. I filled you with new hope
and new life.
All is clean and good now, dear one.
All things that are Mine
are yours.

As God's loving servants, you live in joyous freedom from the power of sin. So consider the benefits you now enjoy—you are brought deeper into the experience of true holiness that ends with eternal life! For sin's meager wages is death, but God's lavish gift is life eternal, found in your union with our Lord Jesus, the Anointed One.

ROMANS 6:22-23 TPT

August 7

Today, take special care
of the words you speak.
Make your speech wise
and allow Me
to remove old habits
of negative talking.
Allow Me to breathe
words of life
into your mouth
like apples of gold.
Today begins change
and turn-around
in your communication
with others.

Let every word you speak be drenched with grace and tempered with
truth and clarity. For then you will be prepared to give a respectful
answer to anyone who asks about your faith.

COLOSSIANS 4:6 TPT

August 8

I want you strong.
I want you to be filled with faith.
I don't want you to worry
about money.
I want you to know
that I'm helping you
and that I know your needs.
It's important that you trust Me
and that you have faith in My Word.
Work at prospering your soul
and watch how I'll prosper your health
and pocket book.
Be strong in Me
and in the power of My presence.
Stop complaining.
I want you to be
a powerful person of faith.

"I am the Bread of Life.
Come every day to me and you will never be hungry.
Believe in me and you will never be thirsty."

JOHN 17:23 TPT

August 9

Be prepared
to be gleefully surprised
as I release the blessings
into your life that you've prayed for.
I've told you that I'm an ever-present help
in your time of need
and trouble, and I want you
to understand the very same Spirit
that raised Me from the dead
lives in you. You're enveloped
in My wise presence,
so never be afraid to ask
and keep on asking.
I hear you and I answer you.
Get ready!

Let us then approach God's throne of grace with confidence, so that
we may receive mercy and find grace to help us in our time of need.

HEBREWS 4:16 NIV

August 10

Today, if things come against you
to cause you anxiety and trepidation,
know that you have strength
within you to withstand all negativity.
I'm giving you perfect peace
and confidence in who you are.
The words to speak are already inside you
as I am with you. Trust Me today.
Don't allow yourself
to become agitated or nervous
because all is well. I promise.

Don't be pulled in different directions or worried about a thing.
Be saturated in prayer throughout each day,
offering your faith-filled requests before God
with overflowing gratitude. Tell him every detail of your life,
then God's wonderful peace that transcends human understanding,
will make the answers known to you through Jesus Christ.

PHILIPPIANS 4:6-7 TPT

August 11

When you feel pressured by people,
or when you feel opposition,
that's the time to stand up in the maturity
of your soul and make use
of your spiritual gifts.
Exercise the self-control
established in your soul by My Spirit.
Don't be careless with your
emotions. If you follow the emotional currents
of the atmosphere around you,
you'll fall prey to pressures,
conflict, and disagreement,
but when you exercise your holy gifts
of spiritual discernment accompanied
by wisdom and patience,
you'll champion all situations you face today.

Grace was given to each one of us according to the measure of Christ's gift. Therefore it says, "When he ascended on high he led a host of captives, and he gave gifts to men."

Ephesians 4:7-8 esv

August 12

Don't follow the negative current
of your transient feelings
without curbing yourself,
pulling back and listening to Me
for some holy, anointed guidance.
Quiet your soul today and listen.
I'll give you words to say,
and I'll show you the way to act.
The answers are all within you
by My Spirit.
If you allow your feelings
to leap ahead of you like spunky puppies,
you won't hear a word I tell you.
Listen for My gentle voice within telling you,
"This is the way, My child, walk in it."

Know this, my beloved brothers:
let every person be quick to hear,
slow to speak, slow to anger.

JAMES 1:19 ESV

August 13

Don't think for a minute that anyone can take
anything away from you that I'm not aware of.
I'm the one who owns everything you possess!
Have you not given your life to Me?
Am I not the one who owns
all there is on earth and in heaven,
as well as what's yours?
Do you think that anything
could be stolen from you that's not stolen from Me?
I see and know all things. Nothing escapes My eye.
I've given you spiritual gifts no one can take from you.
Use your gifts. All vengeance is Mine,
and you, dear child, just use your spiritual gifts!

There are different kinds of gifts,
but the same Spirit distributes them.

1 CORINTHIANS 12:4 NIV

August 14

When you feel overwhelmed
and overworked,
I'm here to ease your load.
Nothing should overwhelm you in your life
because I'm your Savior who saves you
from wearing yourself out
and becoming exhausted.
Drop the exalted expectations
you have of yourself.
Respect your own boundaries
and limitations. Do your work
dutifully and prayerfully,
and I'll do the rest
because I love you and I want you
to live a healthy, prosperous, long life.

May the LORD reward your work,
and your wages be full from the LORD, the God of Israel,
under whose wings you have come to seek refuge.

RUTH 2:12 NASB

August 15

I'm giving you My heart at this moment,
and I'm also giving you My mind.
These are enough for you
to do the work of prospering your soul.
Look at all that I've given you.
You won't prosper in your life
until your soul prospers.
I tell you, work on the elements
of your soul which means
your mind, your emotions, and your will.
Fill these with the kiss of God.
Don't allow yourself to flail about
in the dark, dismal back alleys
of an undeveloped, hungry soul.
The riches you need at this time
are the riches of a wholly nurtured soul.

Beloved friend, I pray that you are prospering in every way and that
you continually enjoy good health, just as your soul is prospering.

3 John 1:2 TPT

August 16

When the days seem dark around you
and the world around you looks frightening,
look up.
I'll never leave My children
to fend for themselves in the world.
I'll never leave you to work out
your life's mission by yourself.
I've sent you My Holy Spirit
to guide and instruct you
in good times of security and plenty,
and in hard, dangerous times of lack.
Become accustomed to the leading
of My Holy Spirit.
Maintain an intimate relationship
with My Holy Spirit,
for we are one and the same.
Move ahead today with new courage and resolve.
Know that you're more than a conqueror in Me,
and no events of the world around you
can rob your inheritance in Me.
You're alive for this moment in history.

Even in the midst of all these things, we triumph over them all,
for God has made us to be more than conquerors,
and his demonstrated love is our glorious victory over everything!

ROMANS 8:37 TPT

August 17

I have stored up for you hidden manna,
which is secret nourishment from heaven.
I'm empowering you
with the anointing of My Holy Spirit.
I've watched your hard work and your patience.
I know that you've carefully examined your life,
and given all of yourself to Me.
I know how you suffer for Me,
and I know your many concerns.
Heavenly riches and blessings are yours,
for you've remained strong.
You have a royal position
in My kingdom and you're embraced
by the glory of God in all you do for Me.
Remain strong and true to Me.
You have many rewards coming.

To everyone who is victorious I will let him feast on the hidden manna
and give him a shining white stone. And written upon the white stone is
inscribed his new name, known only to the one who receives it.

REVELATION 2:17 TPT

August 18

Delight yourself in Me.
Feed yourself by reading and meditating
on My Word and I'll bring to pass
everything you ache to see
take place in your life.
I'm building your character.
It's in My Word that you'll come
to a clearer understanding
of who I am and how your personality
must reflect Mine.
You can associate with certain people
and become like them,
or you can associate with Me
and become like Me.

Study this Book of Instruction continually. Meditate on it day and night
so you will be sure to obey everything written in it. Only then will you
prosper and succeed in all you do.

JOSHUA 1:8 NLT

August 19

In utter simplicity and candid honesty,
come to Me today.
Never complain to Me
about what I haven't given you
because I've given you everything
you need for today.
Sometimes you can't see clearly.
Look with your spiritual eyes
and see the glory
that lies before you and in you!
Cast aside your questions
and bewilderments. My arms have been
outstretched for you to climb into Me.
I've opened up to you all the wonders
of heaven and all the wisdom
you need to live courageously and victoriously
all of your days on the earth.

My son, give me your heart,
and let your eyes observe my ways.

PROVERBS 23:26 ESV

August 20

I've gathered you in My arms
and I'll never let you go.
There's nothing I hold back
from you. If you'll pay attention
to My Word and listen to My voice,
I'll continue to lead you forward
on the perfect path
I've designed just for you.
Set your affections on Me
and keep them there. Center your attention
where it belongs.
When your heart and mind are fixed
on your purpose on earth,
all doubts are automatically
removed and the way is made clear.
Move forward today in your calling
and you'll see what I mean.

Beloved ones, listen to this instruction.
Open your heart to the revelation of this mystery that I share with you.

PSALM 78:1 TPT

August 21

As you labor at your project
I'm with you,
and it's your heart's overflow
that I enjoy most.
Your project will be completed,
but consider what you've gained
inwardly with each hour of labor.
I look for the waft of heaven
overflowing from a courageous,
grateful heart.
Take pleasure in your work
and in your skills as I do.
Be happy.
Who accomplishes the job?
You, or you in Me?

They replied, "So what should we do if we want to do God's work?"
Jesus answered, "The work you can do for God starts
with believing in the One he has sent."

John 6:28-29 TPT

August 22

I learned obedience through suffering
and self-discipline.
Can you do any less?
My apostle, Paul, told you
to endure difficulties as a good soldier
because everything that coddles
and babies the flesh and weakens the spirit.
I want you strong!
It's My desire to bless you
with a double portion for your endurance
and your courage.
Today, lay aside every weighty complaint.
Run with patience the course I've set before you
and you won't get tired.
I'm strengthening you and running beside you.

We point to you as an example of unwavering faith for all the churches
of God. We boast about how you continue to demonstrate unflinching
endurance through all the persecutions and painful trials you are
experiencing.

2 Thessalonians 1:4 tpt

August 23

I often call you to a prayer watch
in the night hours.
When you awake at three a.m.,
roll up from your slumber and pray.
Pour out your praise, your love, and worship Me.
My Holy Spirit will show you
how to pray as you ought.
The time is short. The storm is gathering fast.
When you see dark clouds gathered in the sky,
you know a storm is approaching, so I tell you
discern the events of the time,
which currently shape the history of the world,
and keep your eyes keen.
Know when I wake you in the night hours to pray,
it's a high calling reserved for My captains of faith.

My soul yearns for you in the night,
my spirit within me earnestly seeks you.
For when your judgments are in the earth,
the inhabitants of the world learn righteousness.

Isaiah 26:9 NRSV

August 24

I'm your life.
Needless burdens only press on your spirit
and interfere with the blessing
that wait to overtake you.
Much remains to be accomplished
with the work I've given you
to do, and it's going to prosper
and burgeon far beyond
your expectations as My Spirit
continues to help you.
Be patient and do one task at a time
while you keep steadily moving forward.
All things are working together
for good, so keep your eye fixed
on the goal and don't be side-tracked.
Glorious consummation awaits you.

My dear brothers and sisters, stand firm. Let nothing move you.
Always give yourselves fully to the work of the Lord,
because you know that your labor in the Lord is not in vain.

1 Corinthians 15:58 niv

August 25

Live each day as though
it were your first day on earth.
Be filled with wonder and gratitude.
Seize every opportunity to honor Me,
for no situation will occur
the same way twice
and the opportunities of today
won't match those of tomorrow.
The moments count.
Live as though you're the first
to enter every open door and
step into each new adventure.
I'll give you the necessary wisdom
and grace for every action you take.
I'm helping you overcome all self-doubt.
I made the day for you.

Let the heavens be glad, and the earth rejoice!
Tell all the nations, "The Lord reigns!"

1 Chronicles 16:31 nlt

August 26

I'm able to help you
in the midst of every human experience
that includes frustrations and trials.
Pain and suffering are a part
of the walk on earth,
but you, My child, must rise above
every tendency to fall
into the sins of self-pity, self-reproach,
resentment, or depression.
I know it's not easy. But the same grace
I promised to the apostle Paul
to help him bear his afflictions
is the same grace I give to you.
Be strong today. You are so loved.

Can anything ever separate us from Christ's love? Does it mean he no
longer loves us if we have trouble or calamity, or are persecuted,
or hungry, or destitute, or in danger, or threatened with death?

ROMANS 8:35 NLT

August 27

Today, don't be afraid to step out
and stand up
for that which is right and good.
Don't be afraid
to leave behind something
that you've valued in the past
but you know is no longer right
or good for you.
Stand up and be strong, child.
Throw fear from you
as you would shrug a bug
from your sleeve.
Treasures of great joy
lie ahead in your future
when you're brave and do what is right.

Yes, everything else is worthless when compared with the infinite
value of knowing Christ Jesus my Lord. For his sake I have discarded
everything else, counting it all as garbage, so that I could gain Christ

PHILIPPIANS 3:8 NLT

August 28

I'm always sending you
spiritual signs to encourage you,
which you must be
spiritually attentive to receive.
Expect confirmation
that you're going in the right direction.
Often this confirmation will come
in the form of opposition, hardship, and trials.
I want you stronger in your faith,
and your faith is
growing,
growing,
growing,
so press on, dear one,
because I'm also sending you
milestones of blessings along the way.
My Spirit of truth is in you
to help you every hour of the day.
You're at the point of break-through!

**Be strong in the Lord
and in the power of His might.**

EPHESIANS 6:10 NKJV

August 29

It's not difficult to learn
how to live a full
and abundant life in Me.
I'm renewing your mind,
so all your anxious thoughts
will evaporate
in their tracks
as you build new pathways
of thinking.
Experience My joy
in your soul today.
I'm guiding you every minute.

**I will rejoice in the LORD!
I will be joyful in the God of my salvation!**

HABAKKUK 3:18 NLT

August 30

It's not through your obedience
that you're forgiven, it's by My blood.
I paid for your forgiveness,
for your peace of mind,
and for the healing of your body
by the bloody beating I took,
and My death on the cross.
You can trust Me for the healing
and care of your soul
and body as you come to Me
for all your needs today.
You're being transformed into My image
moment-by-moment,
even when you aren't aware of it,
so don't fret over minor or major set-backs.
Start again and carry on!
I hold nothing back from you
when you are open and real with Me.

Let the wicked change their ways and banish the very thought of doing
wrong. Let them turn to the Lord that he may have mercy on them.
Yes, turn to our God, for he will forgive generously.

Isaiah 55:7 nlt

August 31

Every believer has serious inner work to do,
the work of changing old,
depressing thought patterns to new,
positive, spirit-filled thoughts.
This is work accomplished through Me
and My Holy Spirit.
It's the work of building your beautiful faith.
If you're tempted to grumble,
change your negative thought patterns
to My thought patterns.
I never told you this life
would be easy to navigate with a lazy,
"whatever" way of thinking.
Tell yourself the truth!
It's not laborious.
I tell you today to listen to My Spirit,
look to My Word and let Me cheer you up!

"When He, the Spirit of truth, has come, He will guide you into all truth; for He will not speak on His own authority, but whatever He hears He will speak; and He will tell you things to come."

JOHN 16:13 NKJV

SEPTEMBER

"I have loved you with an everlasting love;

Therefore with lovingkindness

I have drawn you."

JEREMIAH 31:3 NKJV

September 1

Your soul is the entire spectrum
of your human emotions.
Your soul is the entire realm
of your thinking human mind.
Your soul is your will,
which is the power within you
to make choices
and exercise human discipline.
Your soul is not your spirit.
When David prayed, "Bless the Lord, O my soul,"
he was addressing himself adamantly
and ordering his human intellect,
his human emotions, and his human will
to be a blessing to God.
If you are to prosper, as your soul prospers,
you must do the same.

Bless the LORD, O my soul;
and all that is within me, bless His holy name!

PSALM 103:1 NKJV

September 2

I'm leading you to a higher place at this time
and I'm disciplining you.
Be glad that you're so carefully watched over,
for you are continuing
to grow tall spiritually every day.
I want you to be fruitful and multiply,
and I want to show you how to do that.
Everybody has a different path,
and your path is yours alone.
No one else is called to be who I've called you to be.
The problems that you face are small
compared to the glory that you have within you.
Keep your eyes on Me,
and never on the problems surrounding you.
They're dust in the wind.
You're a pillar in My kingdom.

God sends angels with special orders to protect you wherever you go,
defending you from all harm.
If you walk into a trap, they'll be there for you
and keep you from stumbling.

PSALM 91:11-12 TPT

September 3

Be wise regarding your soul
because there's absolutely no profit
in gaining the whole world
if it means losing your soul.
Man can do nothing to you
to steal heaven from your soul.
Guard your soul, love your soul,
and love Me.
This is all you need to prosper.
Never be afraid or ashamed
of who you are in Me
because I will always support you.
Today, be aware of heaven reigning in your soul.

"What do you benefit if you gain the whole world
but lose your own soul?"

MARK 8:36 NLT

September 4

Be merciful today.
When I was on the earth
I was asked to pass judgment
on a woman caught in adultery
and I told the crowd of accusers,
"Whoever is without sin, cast the first stone."
The stones were dropped
because no one on earth is without sin
except Me.
I was qualified to throw a rock
that day because I was the one
without sin. But, darling one,
I don't condemn or cast stones.
I embrace with love, wisdom,
and forgiveness. That's the mercy
I love you with, and that's the mercy
that lives in you to give, too.

**"Let any one of you who is without sin
be the first to throw a stone at her."**

JOHN 8:7 NIV

September 5

Don't allow your prayers
to be worry events or vexing,
hand-wringing, pleading sessions.
So many of My children lift up
prayers accompanied by the smell
of anxiety and fear.
When you pray, pray with faith
because it's the sweet aroma
of faith that delights Me to answer.
Pray knowing that My love for you
is everlasting and true,
and that your heartfelt, earnest prayers
have tremendous power.
Pray knowing My promises are eternal.
Be courageous today
and ask Me for big things.

Confess and acknowledge how you have offended one another
and then pray for one another to be instantly healed,
for tremendous power is released through the passionate,
heartfelt prayer of a godly believer!

JAMES 5:16 TPT

September 6

You live in the secret place
of the Most High.
Think of yourself today
as blessed with immeasurable goodness
surrounding you.
You're the head and not the tail;
you're on top of things, not beneath things
like a dog under the table.
You're above all negative
and worrisome circumstances.
I call you righteous and this means
you're good, moral, blameless, honest,
upright, and honorable just like Me!
I've given you My righteousness
so that in all you do, you please
and bless Me, and in blessing Me,
you bless the world.

The Lord will make you the head, not the tail. If you pay attention to the commands of the Lord your God that I give you this day and carefully follow them, you will always be at the top, never at the bottom.

DEUTERONOMY 28:13 NIV

September 7

I'm in no hurry,
I don't rush.
Don't think
I'm taking
My time with you
to teach you a lesson.
You're living
in My perfect favor.
I'm pleased with you,
and My timing
is right on target.
You'll see
the reasons today.

There is an appointed time for everything.
And there is a time for every event under heaven.

ECCLESIASTES 3:1 NASB

September 8

I'm renewing your mind today
so all your anxious thoughts
will diminish, and you'll feel the joy
of Me deep in your soul.
I'm guiding you and helping you
make the decisions that lie before you.
I don't want you worrying
about money and paying bills.
I know your needs before you do.
It's important that you trust Me!
The prosperous soul brings forth
material blessings. Stop complaining
about money and be led by faith.
I want you to be filled and motivated
with your uncompromising faith.
It's not difficult to live
a full and abundant life
when your soul is fed by faith.

**We can be sure that we know him
if we obey his commandments.**

1 John 2:3 NLT

September 9

Don't be upset by My discipline.
It requires your effort, but it's not that difficult
to handle. It does mean
you'll need to make some changes
which you may not want to make.
But be glad that you're loved enough
for Me to see you reach your best.
Pull yourself up in faith and don't hold on
to the bad habits that rob you
of the life you are meant to live.
Don't shrink back.
Your spiritual growth is a continual process
and the problems you face are small
compared to the glory you have within you.
Keep your eyes on the goal today,
and not on the problems.

All discipline seems to be more pain than pleasure at the time,
yet later it will produce a transformation of character, bringing a
harvest of righteousness and peace to those who yield to it.

HEBREWS 12:11 TPT

September 10

Today, if you become distracted
and confused with too much work
or too much going on
around you, take a moment
to breathe and remember
who you are and who I am.
I've given you
a sound mind to reason out
every disturbance that comes your way.
The problems of the world
are not your problems.
I give you authority to pray
in My name that My will be done.
You can be confident I'll do
as I promise, so allow all confusion
to fall from you and trust Me.

God has not given us a spirit of fear,
but of power and of love and of a sound mind.

2 TIMOTHY 1:7 NKJV

September 11

You'll always
find your way to Me
for you're never
without Me. I'm with you
always even when
you're far from Me.
I'm here beside you now
to remove all
vestige of distance
between us.
Nothing is too hard
for Me, and nowhere
is too far away for you to find Me.

It's impossible to disappear from you
or to ask the darkness to hide me,
for your presence is everywhere,
bringing light into my night.

PSALM 139:11 TPT

September 12

Can anything be hidden that I'm unable to see?
Does My presence not fill the heavens
and the earth?
Do you think I don't know
everything that goes on in the earth?
I see and know everything.
Nothing escapes My eye.
I'm no further away from you
on earth than I am from
My home in heaven, for I'm
everywhere at once.
I see all and know all.
I see every corner of heaven
and I see every corner of earth
at all times.
Never underestimate
Who I am or compare Me to any other.

"Can a man hide himself in secret places
so that I cannot see him?" declares the LORD.
"Do I not fill heaven and earth?"

JEREMIAH 23:24 ESV

September 13

I'm fully in the world, not just a part of it.
I'm immense, and I'm immeasurable.
I'm all time, and I'm above time.
I'm in all places, and I'm above
limitation by anything. I'm infinite.
My beloved children who suffer
at the hand of evildoers and hate-mongers
are precious gifts to the world
and to Me, and all of eternity.
Do you think I turn My face
in the presence of evil or when
I see My children persecuted?
I don't turn My face. Never think
the devil can erase Me.
Understand this today: when evil abounds,
My grace is a tsunami!
Watch the signs. I'm returning soon.

The earth is the LORD's, and everything in it,
the world, and all who live in it.

PSALM 24:1 NIV

September 14

If it's difficult for you
to conceive of the glory of heaven,
know that those
who are persecuted for My sake
experience My glory without measure.
My children who rise above
unthinkable suffering
are ushered into My presence
with much pomp, glory, and heaven's joy.
Celebrated homage is given
to My brave, noble, and innocent lambs.
You may ask why I don't put an end to evil.
Remember, I told you I have given all humans
the power of choice.
Evil is a choice. Love is a privilege.
But keep watch, dear child, I'm coming soon.
Stay solid on your journey.

"Blessed are those who are persecuted because of righteousness,
for theirs is the kingdom of heaven."

MATTHEW 5:10 NIV

September 15

I can't be measured by time,
and I can't be limited by place.
Your body and soul are finite,
and you fill but one space at a time.
My Spirit within you is infinite,
and I am infinite.
I fill all. I fill the heights of the heavens
and the bottom of the deepest point
of the world. I'm beyond all time and space.
All things are subject to Me.
I'm present with all things
and I'm right here with you now, My dear child.
Your face is ever before Me.
Be prepared to move into unknown territory
in the near future as you step into
new possibilities beyond what you've planned.
Your faith will expand to new heights
as I take you on your new journey.

The Son radiates God's own glory and expresses the very character of
God, and he sustains everything by the mighty power of his command.

HEBREWS 1:3 NLT

September 16

I'm intimate with all My creation,
and there's not the least particle
of any creature created by Me
in which the marks
of My glory and goodness
are not seen.
My goodness attends to all.
I'm the breaking of light
from the sun at dawn
and parade of dark at dusk.
I'm everywhere there is life,
and here I am with you.
Take a break to share
our intimacy.

"You are worthy, our Lord and God,
to receive glory, honor, and power,
for you created all things,
and by your plan they were created and exist."

REVELATION 4:11 TPT

September 17

I want you to enjoy My presence
because I'm present
in all My creation.
I've created all things
and I care for all things.
I offer you My friendship every day
to be loved and cherished by Me.
and to love Me back.
I've called you to take care
of the natural things
of the world. All is in your hands.
I'm calling you to reach out today
and expand the boundaries of your heart.

"Oh that you would bless me and enlarge my border, and that your hand might be with me, and that you would keep me from harm so that it might not bring me pain!"

1 Chronicles 4:10 esv

September 18

Don't fret yourself over the work of evil doers
and the evil they inflict on the world. Instead, pray.
I call continually to the lost children of darkness
who destroy and murder for the devil's
entertainment. My arms are open
in forgiveness and longing
for the captive slaves of hatred
to be set free. I turn no one away
who comes to Me. And you, dear child,
you, whom I call My own darling,
dearly loved and cherished,
I share My heart with you.
My omnipotence and omnipresence
are providential. You're always with Me.
Pray for divine justice. My will be done.

**Do not fret because of those who are evil
or be envious of those who do wrong.**

PSALM 37:1 NIV

September 19

I've given you great freedom
in your walk with Me.
I've sent you a counselor
and a guide in My Holy Spirit,
and you're free to live
according to the choices
that you make. I acted freely
when I was on the earth
and gave My life voluntarily,
following the promise of the Father.
If I forced you to make the choices I want,
you wouldn't be free.
Choices that you make,
if made by force, can't be called love
because there'd be no deep gratification
in those choices.
When you love Me freely, you'll consciously
and unconsciously choose that which is good.

**"Today I ask heaven and earth to be witnesses.
I am offering you life or death, blessings or curses.
Now, choose life! Then you and your children may live."**

DEUTERONOMY 30:19-20 NCV

September 20

I'd like you to think as My apostle Paul
admonished–to be humble
and to consider everyone else
more important than yourself.
Today, consider what things
are weighing you down
and obscuring your calling
to love others as I love them.
What ideas about yourself
are holding you back?
Today, come into My arms of grace
and let Me free you from everything
that binds you from loving others
without fear of being hurt.

Because of the privilege and authority God has given me, I give each
of you this warning: Don't think you are better than you really are.
Be honest in your evaluation of yourselves, measuring yourselves
by the faith God has given us.

ROMANS 12:3 NLT

September 21

You don't know the vastness
of your own soul.
I want you to know your soul.
I want you to know
the power of your emotions
and of your mind.
I want you to know
that you've been
created in My image,
and the characteristics
that you have in your soul
are like the great omnipotent,
omnipresent, omniscience
of the God who loves you.

I pray that you will continually experience the immeasurable greatness
of God's power made available to you through faith. Then your lives will
be an advertisement of this immense power as it works through you!

EPHESIANS 1:19 TPT

September 22

Today, show special respect to My servants,
the men and women who serve Me
and give liberally of themselves
with little reward for your sake.
Be the one who is sensitive
to My servants' needs.
I've called them to serve you,
and I've called you to honor them.
These chosen, unsung workers of God.
They live to love, bless,
and nourish you on your holy path.
They make sacrifices that you'll never see.
You honor Me when you honor them.

It is a proof of your faith. Many people will praise God because you obey the Good News of Christ—the gospel you say you believe— and because you freely share with them and with all others.

2 CORINTHIANS 9:13 NCV

September 23

Don't be hard on yourself
if you think you fail Me in your walk.
You can't go too far from Me.
You can't run to the ends of the world
and not find Me waiting there for you.
Come, let Me look at you.
Give Me a smile.
Every day is a new day.
Every moment is an opportunity
for better choices.
Give Me your will and allow your will
to be inundated with the passion
of wanting to please Me, and then you'll know
the greatest happiness
any human being can experience.
Authentic bliss is knowing
you're stuck to Me forever.

**"I give to them the gift of eternal life
and they will never be lost
and no one has the power
to snatch them out of my hands."**

JOHN 10:28 TPT

September 24

I want you to relax.
It's not My will that you
have no place to pause
and rest during hectic days
of busyness. Sleep is good,
but I want to give your body
and mind a sweet time-out,
where you have fun
and laugh and play.
Your work is not meant
to be grievous,
and that's why
I've given you My Spirit
to live in you
and give you My peace
and My rest.
Take time out today for you.

**I will satisfy the weary,
and all who are faint I will replenish.**

JEREMIAH 31:25 NRSV

September 25

Expect things to get much better.
You have a perfect
iron-clad covenant with Me,
and true and infallible promises
in My blood that can't be broken.
Expect the coming days
to be better than the last.
Favor responds to the gifts
of My Spirit and you've been faithful,
trusting Me
and exercising your gifts.
You're attracting goodness
and blessing beyond measure.
Expect a new unleashing
of My favor.

"This is My blood of the covenant,
which is poured out for many for forgiveness of sins."

Matthew 26:28 NASB

September 26

It's time to discard all pursuits
that lead nowhere.
I'm the somewhere you crave.
I'm the someone,
the only someone you need.
I'm the one who loves you eternally,
and whose blessing is forever.
Those who think they've found success
but are left with empty, broken souls
have fallen into an abyss of their own choosing.
Your soul was meant to be filled with Me,
not with godless, vain pursuits.
Let Me direct your path and guide you in all things.
Your life will become rich with peace and joy.
I'm your everything.

The end of the matter; all has been heard.
Fear God and keep his commandments,
for this is the whole duty of man.
For God will bring every deed into judgment,
with every secret thing, whether good or evil.

ECCLESIASTES 12:13-14 ESV

September 27

My hand of instruction and direction
is always extended to you.
When you plunge forward
doing good works before consulting Me,
you'll wear yourself out
floundering in waters, going nowhere.
Don't neglect the quiet moments
alone with Me as you wait for My leading.
It may seem I'm taking My time,
or you may think I've passed you by,
but I have never for a second
taken My eye off you.
Don't be in a hurry to enter pleasant
waters not meant for you.
Show Me you can wait with a joyful heart
because you'll see that everything
is perfect in My timing.

Lord, you are so good to me,
so kind in every way and ready to forgive,
for your grace-fountain keeps overflowing,
drenching all your lovers who pray to you.

PSALM 86:5 TPT

September 28

The first and greatest benefit
of your relationship
with Me is forgiveness.
Sin that once separated us
separates us no more.
I multiply My forgiveness
in your life.
I forgive sins of the heart,
of the mouth, and all sins of omission
and commission.
The sweetness of our relationship
is founded on My sacrifice
and divine, perfect love.
Let nothing tarnish
or fragment our sweet communication.

How happy and fulfilled are those
whose rebellion has been forgiven,
those whose sins are covered by blood.

PSALM 32:1 TPT

September 29

It's My desire
to make your life better every day.
Getting better and growing
in Me is in your spiritual DNA.
You're designed by Me
to grow spiritually,
and to prosper physically,
emotionally, financially,
and in all your relationships.
Your path is going to become
easier and sweeter in the coming days.
Expect much favor and act on it.
You can't offer happiness to someone else
until you have it yourself.

The path of the righteous is like the light of dawn,
that shines brighter and brighter until the full day.

PROVERBS 4:18 NASB

September 30

Today, be an encouragement to others.
Inspire peace and compassion.
Bring light into the darkness for those
who are in need of illumination.
Choose to embrace wisdom and truth
to both friend and stranger.
Choose to be a peacemaker.
Choose to befriend those who
are different from you,
and offer understanding and warmth
where there is coldness and hostility.
Be a warm, welcoming blanket
to a calloused, indifferent world.

Be kind to one another, tender-hearted, forgiving each other,
just as God in Christ also has forgiven you.

EPHESIANS 4:32 NASB

OCTOBER

He who dwells in the secret place

of the Most High

Shall abide under the shadow

of the Almighty.

PSALM 91:1 NKJV

October 1

Watch My favor multiply
every day as you grow
in spiritual strength.
I am your Lord,
and all glory, honor,
majesty, and splendor
belong to Me,
both now and forever.
Knowing this
is your salvation
and the soul of your favor.

To the King that rules forever,
who will never die, who cannot be seen,
the only God, be honor and glory forever and ever.

1 TIMOTHY 1:17 NCV

October 2

There's a lion in you;
don't forget that.
You're a force to be reckoned with.
You walk with Me and I am
the most powerful force
in all of creation.
Don't hold back today.
Be brave enough to release
the strength that lives in you.
This takes courage.
And I give you that courage.

You, however, are not in the realm of the flesh but are in the realm of
the Spirit, if indeed the Spirit of God lives in you. And if anyone does
not have the Spirit of Christ, they do not belong to Christ.

ROMANS 8:9 NIV

October 3

Real intimacy, dear one,
is when you look into the eyes
of the one who looks for you
and loves you.
When you look at Me,
you must see with your spiritual eyes,
for that which is seen is temporary,
but the eyes of your spirit can see
into that which ordinary human eyes cannot.
Look at Me looking at you.
What do you see?

The Lord sees all we do;
he watches over his friends day and night.
His godly ones receive the answers they seek
whenever they cry out to him.

PSALM 34:15 TPT

October 4

I've searched
throughout the whole earth
for one like you
to show Myself
strong in.
Your happily-ever-after
has come.
Live today
as the best day of your life.

We know that the Son of God has made our understanding come alive so that we can know by experience the One who is true. And we are in him who is true, God's Son, Jesus Christ—the true God and eternal life!

1 John 5:20 TPT

October 5

Come apart from yourself and see
the answers you've been
requiring of Me are here for you today.
Don't be discouraged.
Yesterday is gone, and now you're going
to see Me move in mighty
power on your behalf.
Relinquish your fears to Me now.

Come out from them, and be separate from them, says the Lord,
and touch nothing unclean; then I will welcome you.

2 Corinthians 6:17 NRSV

October 6

Change is coming.
You're going to see
adjustments in your personal
and professional life this month
because I am blessing you with favor.
You're going to see progress
and successful completion.
You're going to have favor
to be the influence
I've called you to be.

Some trust in chariots, and some in horses;
But we will remember the name of the LORD our God.
They have bowed down and fallen;
But we have risen and stand upright.

PSALM 20:7-8 NKJV

October 7

That which you once thought
was impossible
is now becoming
readily possible.
Keep your expectations high
and don't settle for less.
Despise not the small things,
nor the seemingly insignificant.
Everything you touch
is important to Me.

Do not despise these small beginnings,
for the Lord rejoices to see the work begin,
to see the plumb line in Zerubbabel's hand.

ZECHARIAH 4:10 NLT

October 8

All creation is important to Me,
and as you become more aware
of this, you'll treat the world
around you with much more
loving care. Nothing is insignificant
on earth to Me—nothing.
As I love you, I love what you love.
Walking with Me, you make
the world a more beautiful place.

Then the LORD God took the man and put him into the garden of Eden
to cultivate it and keep it.

GENESIS 2:15 NASB

October 9

You ask to know more
of Me and to be closer to Me.
I'm answering you today
and revealing Myself
to you in a fresh, new manner.
You're going to find Me
in the depths of your prayers
and in your steadfast faith.
Find Me in My Word,
where I live to show you
more of who you are in Me,
and how I treasure everything
about you.

He showed you these things so you would know
that the LORD is God and there is no other.

DEUTERONOMY 4:35 NLT

October 10

You're going to see knowledge of Me increase
throughout the earth
and also in your personal sphere of activity.
You're going to see men and women,
boys and girls coming to Me
and learning quickly
that which other generations
took far longer to grasp.
In this new day the old has passed away
and is tucked in the archives
of heaven's historical society.
Don't be satisfied with the past
and become stagnant in the present.
I'm calling you to increase
with fresh spiritual awareness,
faith and revelation.

"Who would pour fresh, new wine into an old wineskin? Eventually the
wine will ferment and make the wineskin burst, losing everything—the
wine is spilled and the wineskin ruined. Instead, new wine is always
poured into a new wineskin so that both are preserved."

MATTHEW 9:17 TPT

October 11

Speak the words I give you to speak.
Say what I give you to say,
for from your mouth everyone
will hear the passion of your heart,
which I have given you.
You shall be as My mouth.

The faith-righteousness we receive speaks to us in these words of
Moses: "God's living message is very close to you, as close as your own
heart beating in your chest and as near as the tongue in your mouth."

Romans 10:8 TPT

October 12

I've put a new song in your heart
and new spiritual authority
in the words you speak.
I've given you ears to hear
My still, small voice within you.
Listen to the music in your soul
and the words I speak to you.
You'll have excellent
opportunities to show My love
today.

He put a new song in my mouth,
a song of praise to our God.
Many will see and fear,
and put their trust in the LORD.

PSALM 40:3 ESV

October 13

I've given you
My wisdom and knowledge
so you'll teach and give
to others. I'll empower you
with My Spirit to share
what you've been given,
for you've grown in both
natural and spiritual understanding
and this pleases Me.
Your gifts of wisdom and
discernment will open doors
to freedom and new life
for many, so today I'm calling
you to be bold and confident
in your gifts and calling.

They will teach you how to be wise and self-controlled
and will teach you to do what is honest and fair and right.

PROVERBS 1:3 NCV

October 14

You may wonder why I withhold
certain promises instead of rushing
to answer right away.
It's at this moment of questioning
that you must understand deep within
the heart of your mind that I'm God,
I am that I am, and I cannot fail, nor lie.
Every promise is true. The promises
I've made to you are sealed with My blood.
I'll do all that I've promised you.
Take heart.
Hold on.

Here's what I've learned through it all:
Don't give up; don't be impatient;
be entwined as one with the Lord.
Be brave and courageous, and never lose hope.
Yes, keep on waiting—for he will never disappoint you!

PSALM 27:14 TPT

October 15

Today, you can face everything
before you with boldness and confidence,
knowing I've got you covered.
We have an agreement
called the New Covenant
and here's what you're promised,
along with so much more:
forgiveness, eternal life,
and a blessed walk on the earth
with Me empowering you.
Every detail for a happy
and fulfilled life is covered,
and the terms are sealed in My blood.
I gave My life so you can be bold
and prosper in all things.
Today, find much to delight in,
and give your delight to Me
as a thank you gift.

In the same way he took the cup also, after supper, saying,
"This cup is the new covenant in my blood.
Do this, as often as you drink it, in remembrance of me."

1 CORINTHIANS 11:25 NRSV

October 16

Morning by morning
I awaken you to My voice
to prepare you for what's ahead.
Our time together is your nourishment
and the template for life.
If you busy yourself elsewhere,
neglecting our time together,
you risk opening the windows
of your mind to the winds of worldly thought
which blow you to dead-end alleys of defeat.
Come, let Me awaken you every day
with My Word.
I want you to prosper and succeed.

Because of the LORD's great love we are not consumed,
for his compassions never fail.
They are new every morning;
great is your faithfulness.

LAMENTATIONS 3:22-23 NIV

October 17

Today, I'm calling you
to be wise with your time.
I'm calling you to be fruitful
and productive.
I've given you talents
to multiply for My glory
and honor, and I'll bless you
with a sense of fulfillment
as you press in closer to Me
in all things.
You'll be happy and content
with your new achievements,
because as you open your spiritual eyes
wider, you'll see all is good
and you're dearly honored by Me.

You will enjoy the fruit of your labor.
How joyful and prosperous you will be!

PSALM 128:2 NLT

October 18

You run to and fro so concerned about how
you're going to accomplish this and that,
how you'll meet your responsibilities,
how you'll finish, do, achieve;
oh, on and on–
and I'm right here beside you.
Right here!
Yes, dearest one,
I'm here to make the burden light,
and to show you a better,
happier way to accomplish
everything on your plate.
Today, come to Me
and let Me put My arms
around you and calm your anxious mind.
We'll get it all done together.

Pour out all your worries and stress upon him and leave them there,
for he always tenderly cares for you.

1 PETER 5:7 TPT

October 19

Do the work I've called you to do
with all your strength and energy.
I've given you the tongue of the learned
so you can speak words of wisdom
and encouragement to many.
I'm the one who knows what's best for the world
and what's best for you.
No need to try to figure out
how to get ahead because My ways
of promotion are higher
than human ways, and My thoughts
about getting ahead
are divinely higher than human thoughts.
Do what you do for Me.
I've given you knowledge and understanding
in heavenly patterns of faith.
Promotion is ahead for you.

The Sovereign LORD has given me a well-instructed tongue,
to know the word that sustains the weary.
He wakens me morning by morning,
wakens my ear to listen like one being instructed.

ISAIAH 50:4 NIV

October 20

I love it when you're content
with your life and your calling
even when you don't see
the rewards ahead for you.
My blessing is all you need,
and I give you the gift of joy
and fulfillment as you persevere
with a precious, loyal heart
brimming with love.
Nothing can defeat you.
I've spoken it
and I'll also bring it to pass.

All these blessings will come on you and accompany you
if you obey the Lord your God.

Deuteronomy 28:2 niv

October 21

I'm calling you to be skillful in your work
in this day of indifference and apathy.
Whatever you set your hand to do,
do with all your might, and apply yourself
wholly to the task set before you
knowing I walk with you. I'm calling you
to develop the use of your time.
If you are to be proficient in using
your skills and talents, you must know
how to manage your gift of time. I've set you
in a world system with time at its core
to serve you, not the other way around.
Bring your schedule to Me.
You weren't born to be a servant of time.
Time is to be your servant.
Therefore, you must be wise.
Examine the hours allotted each day,
and make careful arrangements to glorify Me.

**Whatever your hand finds to do,
do it with all your might.**
ECCLESIASTES 9:10 NASB

October 22

I'll bless your daily schedule
as you bring your plans
to Me in prayer.
I know that it can seem
there are more tasks than hours,
and other times not enough to do
to fill the hours.
My daily planner for you
is perfect, dear one.
I give you plenty of time to accomplish
all that I have for you to do,
and I give you plenty of rest
to enjoy the fruit of your labor,
to take a breather and have fun.

Within your heart you can make plans for your future,
but the Lord chooses the steps you take to get there.

PROVERBS 16:9 TPT

October 23

I'm manifesting Myself in you.
I'm making you fruitful
and productive for My glory.
I know your schedule,
the decisions you must make,
and the pressures you live with.
I'm working a miracle inside you
giving you internal calm
and serenity in the rush and bustle of your day.
Don't act in haste. Pause for a moment with Me
at your side and listen for My direction.
My Spirit will flow through you perfectly
so you can draw wisdom and strength into the heart
of your mind. I'm teaching you
to be still and to know that I'm God within you.
Don't let your zeal imprison you.
Take your time.

You shall not go out in haste, and you shall not go in flight,
for the LORD will go before you,
and the God of Israel will be your rear guard.

ISAIAH 52:12 ESV

October 24

I want your life
to be fruitful and invigorating.
I want your days
to be inspired and challenged.
I want you to be resourceful
and experience My endless rewards
on a daily basis.
I want you to live in the strength
of your inward reservoir
of My power.
I want you loved all the days
of your life,
and I want My love
to ooze out of you
to a parched, desperate world.
Take everything I have to give you today.

I will put my Spirit in you and move you
to follow my decrees and be careful to keep my laws.

Ezekiel 36:27 niv

October 25

Don't worry.
Because you have pleased Me,
I'll take care of those who oppose you.
I'll divert the intentions
of competitors and adversaries.
If an enemy rushes at you
like a flood, I'll lift up a standard,
a terrifying, holy barrier
driven by the fire of My breath against him.
Your first and only concern
is to seek My kingdom.
Then all the things I've promised you
will be given you.

From the west to the lands of the rising sun,
the glory and the name of Yahweh will be held in highest reverence,
for he will break in as a flooding, rushing river
driven on by the breath of Yahweh!

ISAIAH 59:19 TPT

October 26

Promotion doesn't come
from the world around you or from people.
Your promotion comes from Me.
I have put My hand upon you
and I've raised you up for My purposes.
No one can take My place to promote you.
I've set you on a high place
above power struggles
and ambitious plights.
I've removed you from airs
of self-promotion. Focus yourself
and all your endeavors
on pleasing Me, and I'll keep you
immune to the snapping dragons
of worldly pursuits.
You're going to receive many promotions.

**Whoever gives heed to instruction prospers,
and blessed is the one who trusts in the Lord.**

Proverbs 16:20 niv

October 27

Your enemies
are invisible.
They're the ones
that rob you of your peace
and your inner happiness.
I formed you
to live a life of lasting happiness
through the power of My Holy Spirit
within you.
I'll silence the opposition
if you ask,
and I'll cause your enemies
to be at peace with you
if you stay under the protection
of My Word.

"The LORD will fight for you,
and you have only to keep still."

EXODUS 14:14 NRSV

October 28

Be encouraged today.
You're a blessing and a delight
to Me. Continue on in your calling
until I tell you My purposes have been fulfilled.
Nothing and no one
can move you, hurt you, or destroy you.
Consider all assaults of the enemy
as mere interferences.
I've told you there's not a weapon
formed against you
that'll succeed in its intention.
My Word is true and can't be broken.
I am My Word.
Believe what I tell you, darling one.

"In that coming day no weapon turned against you will succeed.
You will silence every voice raised up to accuse you.
These benefits are enjoyed by the servants of the LORD;
their vindication will come from me. I, the LORD, have spoken!"

ISAIAH 54:17 NLT

October 29

I want to show you
how to handle your finances.
Turn to My Word
and draw near to Me,
for I have much to teach you
about money. I want to show you
how to be a giver of your resources
and multiply what I give you.
I want to show you
how to prosper and live abundantly
in every area of life.
Give–knowing that I'm the Giver
in you. Give, knowing that you
can't out-give Me. When your ways
please and delight Me,
you'll receive back much more
than you give.

Here's my point. A stingy sower will reap a meager harvest, but the
one who sows from a generous spirit will reap an abundant harvest.

2 Corinthians 9:6 TPT

October 30

Look at My heavens
which I've made with My fingers.
See the moon and the stars
which I've created.
I love you more than these.
I've crowned you honorably,
and I've put you in charge of everything
I've created.
I've put everything under your care.
Tell Me, what are you doing
to take care of all that I've given you today?

When I consider Your heavens, the work of Your fingers,
the moon and the stars, which You have ordained;
what is man that You take thought of him,
and the son of man that You care for him?

PSALM 8:3-9 NASB

October 31

Stop talking about your physical problems.
I want you to stop talking to people about your woes,
trying to get their sympathy.
Stop commiserating over the negative.
The trouble you speak of
comes from your adversary.
When you advertise his work,
who are you glorifying? Me?
I'm your loving, giving God,
all powerful and good.
I hold the answers to all your needs.
Talk to Me, dear one,
and let Me calm your troubled heart.
Let Me help you and heal you,
for this is My will.
Every blessing is within you.

"Don't worry or surrender to your fear.
For you've believed in God,
now trust and believe in me also."

JOHN 14:1 TPT

NOVEMBER

The eyes of the LORD run to and fro

throughout the whole earth,

to show Himself strong on behalf of

those whose heart is loyal to Him.

2 CHRONICLES 16:9 NKJV

November 1

You're going to see many scattered things
fall into place this month.
Keep pressing forward
through all clouds of opposition,
and erase your doubts.
I have huge blessings ahead for you.
I'm unstopping the dam that has
kept your soul dry;
your vision will be unclogged
by the clutter of the world around you.
I'm unleashing peace
like a sweet, flowing river
to you, and you'll put
many detached pieces together
beautifully by My Spirit.

I press on toward the goal for the prize
of the heavenly call of God in Christ Jesus.

PHILIPPIANS 3:14 NRSV

November 2

Your emotions are such a beautiful part of you.
I formed you with a broad range
of emotions to reflect My personality.
Your emotions are included
in the holy parcel of your soul,
and it's all a part of My desire
to see eternity in you.
I want to ignite you
with the glory of My personality
alive in you by My Spirit.
Your emotional life is meant
to prosper and radiate
with My presence, and this takes
spiritual training and effort.
I'll help you. Begin by knowing who I am.
Come, beloved, come and know Me
better than yesterday.

It is he whom we proclaim,
warning everyone and teaching everyone in all wisdom,
so that we may present everyone mature in Christ.

EPHESIANS 1:17 NRSV

November 3

There is no barrier thick enough
to separate you from Me, dear one.
There is nothing ferocious
nor violent enough to come between us.
No power, principality, height,
nor depth can separate us.
Do you understand that?
My perfect will for your life
stands forever. Nothing can alter,
smudge or defect My will
and My love for you in any way.
Be blessed today.
I have everything concerning your life
and your destiny in the palm of My hand.

Yes, this is our God, our great God forever.
He will lead us onward until the end, through all time,
beyond death, and into eternity!

PSALM 48:14 TPT

November 4

Yes, there is opposition in your life.
There's a force that opposes
the true beautiful walk I've called you to.
And, dear one, most of the opposition
comes from yourself.
Contention and strife
grip you and drop a black curtain
over the peace in your heart and mind.
Too many things annoy you
and cause you to grind your teeth
in jealous contention.
Sweetheart Mine, look at Me!
I'm the one you need to impress, not them!
What does it matter if another has
what you don't have?
The only one who matters is Me!
I'll lift you from the snares of your fleshly concerns
and restore your peace of mind
if you'll let go–let it all go right now.

Wisdom opens your heart to receive wise counsel,
but pride closes your ears to advice
and gives birth to only quarrels and strife.

PROVERBS 13:10 TPT

November 5

I'm here to instruct you in the way
you should go today.
I'm guiding you with My eye
upon each step you take.
Don't resist My leading.
The horse and the mule are undisciplined
because they have no understanding,
but you, beloved child,
you've been given wisdom
and understanding to bring honor
to the kingdom of God.
Function with confidence
in all you undertake to accomplish today.

Don't be like a horse or donkey,
that doesn't understand.
They must be led with bits and reins,
or they will not come near you.

PSALM 32:9 NCV

November 6

Be glad in the depths of your heart
and know that the earth is filled
with My goodness.
Why do you dwell upon the temporary
and negative happenings around you?
By My Word the heavens were created.
By My Word I created all the host of galaxies,
too numerous for you to count.
By the breath of My mouth
I gathered the waters of the seas.
I'm the author and founder
of the wind, the stars, the sun, and the moon.
All things visible and invisible
were created by Me,
and I've given all to you.

You are worthy, our Lord and God, to receive glory and honor and
power, because you made all things. Everything existed and was made,
because you wanted it.

REVELATION 4:11 NCV

November 7

The skill of listening to your own heart
can be confusing to you
because the human heart is fickle.
No one knows you as I know you.
Your heart speaks a language
known only to Me.
You need Me to understand yourself,
for when the heart thinks pure thoughts,
your vision becomes clear
to see Me for who I am.
I hear and speak
the same language as the pure of heart,
and when your inner world
is settled in Me with a pure heart,
your life will shake as an earthquake,
and you'll be forever changed.
Let it be this day.

"What bliss you experience when your heart is pure!
For then your eyes will open to see more and more of God."

MATTHEW 5:8 TPT

November 8

You weren't created to be self-sufficient.
You were created to trust Me.
You were created to find
your personhood and your sufficiency
in Me. You were created
to depend upon Me to provide
all your needs. How is it that
anyone would settle for rusted metal
going their own way when I offer
imperishable polished gold?
Today, pull back for a moment,
look at yourself and your life,
and then turn everything over to Me.
It's not more money you need,
it's more of Me.

"Your heart will always pursue what you value as your treasure."
MATTHEW 6:21 TPT

November 9

There's no need of yours I can't fulfill.
Don't settle for the lies of the enemy
for a single moment.
The devil lured Adam and Eve
with the deception that they could be
like Me if they ate of the forbidden fruit.
Adam and Eve didn't realize
they already were like Me.
They were created in My image,
as are you.
Today, realize who you are.
Resist the temptation
to be too busy to study
My Word and pray.
Today, shed your self-sufficiency
and prove Me on the earth.

My God shall supply all your need
according to His riches in glory by Christ Jesus.

PHILIPPIANS 4:19 NKJV

November 10

This week you're going to see
a turn-around in your life
and in your circumstances
because you've put your trust in Me.
Your prayers are being answered
in unexpected ways, so begin now
by lifting your heart in praise.
Worship God with all your heart, soul, and strength.
I'm at home in the midst of your praise.
Your thankful heart brings Me joy,
and My joy is your strength.
Know that your spiritual strength
is the result of fearless, persistent trust in Me.
You're being renewed and empowered
by My Spirit, and it's just the beginning.

The LORD is my strength and my shield;
my heart trusts in him, and he helps me.
My heart leaps for joy, and with my song I praise him.

PSALM 28:7 NIV

November 11

I fill you with power
in order for you to serve and help people.
The anointing of the servant of God
isn't for the sake of advancing the servant.
The anointing is for the sake of the people.
I've set you free from selfish,
self-driven desires and goals
in order for you
to love people with a pure heart.
When you love purely,
you'll ask for nothing
except for the joy of giving
that which you've received of Me.
Love people for their benefit, not yours.

Faith comes from hearing the Good News,
and people hear the Good News
when someone tells them about Christ.

ROMANS 10:17 NCV

November 12

To be anointed means to receive a sacred unction
of My Holy Spirit to spiritually know the truth
revealed through Me, and this anointing
is necessary to break off the yokes and burdens
from the necks of people
who cry out for help and deliverance.
I am the way, the truth and the life,
and dear anointed child,
as you make Me known
as all truth, and pray for lost,
hurting souls, you'll see burdens
and yokes broken.
Where there was emptiness, pain, and misery,
new life will now spring forth.

Jesus said to him, "I am the way, the truth, and the life.
No one comes to the Father except through Me."

John 14:6 NKJV

November 13

I'm with you in the journey
you're about to take.
Sense Me walking beside you,
and know that I'm making you
strong. Fix your mind on trusting the plans
I've prepared for you.
Be alert as I guide you
throughout the day, helping you
discern between good and
almost-good, and between that
which seems right but is not.
I'll show you which way to turn
and what to avoid along your path.
You're a blessing to many,
so be wise.

This is what the LORD says— your Redeemer, the Holy One of Israel:
"I am the LORD your God, who teaches you what is best for you, who
directs you in the way you should go."

ISAIAH 48:17 NIV

November 14

I've told you that no weapon formed against you
can succeed in any way in its evil intent,
and now I tell you that joy is the most powerful
and successful tool in the toolkit of your emotions.
Joy is your most powerful spiritual skill,
your most powerful faculty.
Joy–a simple three-letter word
that can change the molecular structure
of your environment.
My joy is your strength.
Be joyful today. Insist on it.
Laugh. Be glad. This time is yours.

Sing for joy in the LORD, O you righteous ones;
praise is becoming to the upright.

PSALM 33:1 NASB

November 15

You worry too much.
Take My yoke upon you because no burden
is cumbersome or difficult for Me to carry.
I never carry around anything heavy.
The world you live in is like a feather
on My eyelash. Nothing oppresses Me.
Turn for a moment, dear child,
and breathe in the truth
of what I'm saying to you.
Pause from your worries and doubts
and rejoice in the blessings
I'm lathering on you.
You're My beloved child
and I love to love you.
Come, let's dance on the troubles
that worry you, and then let's laugh
together and watch them, one by one, disappear.

**The Lord helps the fallen
and lifts those ben beneath their loads.**

Psalm 145:14 NLT

November 16

Your words are important.
They bear much weight;
they're like fire.
The tongue has the power
of life and death.
Another thing: don't allow
any harsh words spoken to you
topple the cathedral of peace in you.
Won't you choose My living presence
in all things concerning you?
Concentrate on the blessed life
you're called to.
With My Holy Spirit in you,
you can't fail.

Don't use foul or abusive language.
Let everything you say be good and helpful,
so that your words will be an encouragement
to those who hear them.

EPHESIANS 4:29 NLT

November 17

I'm wisdom, the only true wisdom,
and today is a day
for you to demonstrate wisdom
in all things you encounter.
When you speak with true wisdom
you reveal what human acumen
and talent can't create.
The wisdom in you, dear one,
is supernatural and a gift
of My Holy Spirit. Use your gift
as I direct you and you'll bring
My kingdom into the atmosphere.
Be discerning and
My blessing will follow you.

A spiritual gift is given to each of us so we can help each other.
To one person the Spirit gives the ability to give wise advice;
to another the same Spirit gives a message of special knowledge.

1 CORINTHIANS 12:7-8 NLT

November 18

The natural human mind
can't begin to perceive
what I've prepared for those who love Me.
No one knows the things of God
except My Spirit,
and therefore, it's My Holy Spirit
who gives illumination and revelation
into everything in your life. You're Mine
and I'm yours, so today
show Me how you'll exercise your spiritual muscles
walking in the power
and wisdom of My Spirit
in all you do.

"What no eye has seen, nor ear heard,
nor the heart of man imagined,
what God has prepared for those who love him."

1 Corinthians 2:9 esv

November 19

I've put My Spirit in you
to help you walk a beautiful
and happy path with Me,
living by My Word,
listening to and obeying
My voice.
I tell you to love
your divinely set-apart walk
with Me as together
we enjoy each other
and accomplish the perfect,
glorious will of the Father.
Today, I'm watching over you
and blessing everything you touch.

**If we live by the Spirit,
let us also walk by the Spirit.**

GALATIANS 5:25 NASB

November 20

To win heaven's prize,
wake up
and take your power
as a child of God.
Never be passive.
Never be complacent.
Be persistent
in your prayers.
Don't give up!
I tell you;
it's persistence
that'll win the prize today.

Let this hope burst forth within you,
releasing a continual joy.
Don't give up in a time of trouble,
but commune with God at all times.

ROMANS 12:12 TPT

November 21

Victories in hard situations
are achieved when you worship
and give Me praise,
earnestly praying that My will be done.
Fast from doubt and all negative thinking.
I tell you to rise up now.
Cast off the bedclothes of slumber.
Open your eyes and your heart
and dress yourself in faith,
trusting Me in your circumstances.
Blessings will abound in your life
with your holy determination
because I'm opening the windows
of heaven to you and enveloping you
with the sweet wind of favor.

How long will you lie there, you sluggard?
When will you get up from your sleep?

PROVERBS 6:9 NIV

November 22

Don't neglect the gift in you.
Kindle the embers of your passion
and set your mind on fire
as you consider the magnitude
of your calling.
Miraculous power awaits you
when you lose yourself
in My purposes.
The flames of your passion
will rise and burst forth,
and you'll see signs and wonders take place.
Darling one, you're going to understand
My joy.

Do not neglect your gift,
which was given you through prophecy
when the body of elders laid their hands on you.

1 Timothy 4:14 niv

November 23

I've said ask and you'll receive.
I've said knock and it'll be opened to you.
If I hadn't wanted it to be true
for you, I wouldn't have said it.
When I make a promise in My Word
it's true and it will come to pass.
You can depend upon My Word utterly.
You've depended on people, and they've
failed you. Individuals fail, institutions fail,
nations fail, philosophies fail, but I cannot fail.
My integrity stands behind My Word.
The throne upon which I'm seated
is the backbone of every word I speak.
Believe that you'll receive
when you ask, and that when you knock,
the doors of My heart will be opened to you.
Be persistent. Keep on keeping on.

"So shall My word be that goes forth from My mouth;
it shall not return to Me void, but it shall accomplish what I please,
and it shall prosper in the thing for which I sent it."

Isaiah 55:11 nkjv

November 24

I want your faith to be alive
and vivacious.
I want your faith drenched in love
and stretching across
the atmosphere touching lives
of everyone you come in contact with.
You weren't born to live a laid-back,
passive life.
You were born to live in the power
of My Word and exercise relentless faith.
I've called you
to be filled with the fire of passion,
undaunted and bold,
fully prepared to move mountains
of any size. I'm so proud of you.

We have the living Word of God, which is full of energy,
and it pierces more sharply than a two-edged sword.

HEBREWS 4:12 TPT

November 25

My strength is your strength.
My life is your life.
I love to share Myself with you.
I love to give you all of Me,
for I've told you all that I have
is yours. What do you need today, little one?
What can I give you today?
Do you need healing in your body?
I'm your healer, for I took your ailments
on the cross with Me.
I was beaten and crucified for your sake,
so you could live a healthy,
renewed, forgiven, full, and abundant life
by My Spirit. The same Spirit that raised Me
from the dead dwells in you as My child.

"The thief comes only to steal and kill and destroy;
I came that they may have life, and have it abundantly."

JOHN 10:10 NASB

November 26

I love walking with you
along the many pathways of your life.
As you talk with Me and tell Me
what you're thinking,
I listen and hold each word
you speak in My heart
where it germinates and then blossoms in fullness.
Never be discouraged if I pause
to answer your petitions. Life brings forth life,
and as you trust Me and wait patiently,
growth is taking place in you. Draw closer to Me
and listen to the heartbeat of heaven.
When your mind is renewed and emptied
of strife and anxious thoughts,
you can hear Me much clearer
because I speak to you continually.
I speak and the entire universe stands still.

"Before they even call out to me, I will answer them;
before they've finished telling me what they need,
I'll have already heard."

ISAIAH 65:24 TPT

November 27

I'm near at hand to bless you.
I am pouring goodness and abundance your way.
I've heard you in the dark night
of spiritual battle, and I'm giving you a fresh revelation
of Myself so you can rise up strong
with a shout of praise. I'm giving you the gift
of seeing through the blackness of deceit
and woeful attacks, and with your eyes
you'll see Me dazzling in light to lead you
through all trials, persecutions, and distress.
I'll never leave you alone.
I am always here. You're Mine,
and what happens to you happens to Me.
I will allow nothing to put a blot on My glory.
Rise up in confidence, dear one.
The battle is won.

Why would I fear the future?
For your goodness and love pursue me all the days of my life.
Then afterward, when my life is through,
I'll return to your glorious presence to be forever with you!

PSALM 23:6 TPT

November 28

I'm eager to talk with you.
In our time together on these pages
you're becoming more beautiful,
like a budding flower. I see you thriving!
As you're more familiar with My character
and My personality, your own character
and personality changes to become like Mine.
Only as you know Me can you become like Me.
Feel My pulse as I open to you the wisdom
of heaven. I'm going to reveal many things
to you that you haven't dreamed of.
I'm giving you the spiritual gifts of wisdom
and knowledge to equip you and light
your mind and heart to the truth.
My Word is the bright lamp guiding you
so you'll never lose your way.

**Joyful is the person who finds wisdom,
the one who gains understanding.**

PROVERBS 3:13 NLT

November 29

I want to teach you the paths of wisdom
and give you insight into My ways
and purposes. Allow Me to suggest new desires
for your heart's consideration,
and a new language of My words
in your mouth. I'll cover you
with the warm protection of My perfect will.
When you choose to follow Me
your life will take on a glow of integrity
that's almost tangible, and people will recognize it.
The world is enriched.
Walk with Me along the vaults
of understanding and let your faith
be deepened today. When it comes to your faith,
never settle for moderation.

I will instruct you and teach you the way you should go;
I will counsel you with my eye upon you.

PSALM 32:8 NRSV

November 30

I'm the master surgeon of the soul,
skilled in its cures, as well as those of the body.
Let Me take care of your health, body, soul, and spirit.
Let Me breathe into your hurts and wounds,
and let Me wash with My blood all your scars.
I'm the Lord who heals you.
I heal you from the inside out.
I remove the blight of yesterday
and the injuries to your soul
and body. I'm the Lord who makes all things new.
Your life is locked inside My heart.
This is where you were born to live,
and where you're forever beautiful.

"You are my Maker, my Mediator, and my Master.
Any good thing you find in me has come from you."

PSALM 16:2 TPT

DECEMBER

"Not by might nor by power,
but by My Spirit,"
says the LORD of hosts.

ZECHARIAH 4:6 NKJV

December 1

I knew you before you were in your mother's womb!
Don't be afraid to tell the truth, no matter
what the consequences.
Lies breed more lies and fester in the muck
of deceit–but the truth stands forever
like a bright beacon, even if the light
stings the eyes. I know your heart,
and I'm the only one
you need to concern yourself with impressing.
When your ways please Me,
I'll make even your enemies be at peace with you.
I want you to be swept away in the power of truth.
Reject and resist the lying ploys of the devil
and he'll flee from you.
I'm everything you need.

It was you who formed my inward parts;
you knit me together in my mother's womb.

PSALM 139:13 NRSV

December 2

Fear is a trap; it's a windowless prison.
I tell you; there's nothing to be afraid of,
for I've built a buttress
of safety around you so the dragons
of defeat can't touch a hair on your head.
I've dispatched angels to watch over you
to keep you from hurting yourself.
The biggest danger you face
at this time is your own fear,
and I'm here to help you
overcome that fear.
See Me as your strong tower of safety.
Hold on tight to My Word
that tells you goodness and mercy
are following you all the days of your life.

The Lord is faithful;
he will strengthen you
and guard you from the evil one.

2 Thessalonians 3:3 nlt

December 3

I see everything, and it's the loving, generous heart
that captures My favor.
Vain arguments and petty fights are foolish intrusions
in the life of a believer, who's called to live
in an attitude of calmness and harmony.
Satisfaction at winning an argument
won't last long if it's the start of a war.
Lack of humility will keep you small
and thwart the full expression of your spiritual gifts.
Be expansive today and accept
the imperfect, the not-so beautiful,
the offensive, and the contrary.
Accept and be at peace.
Remember how I calmed
the raging storm on the Sea of Galilee?
Well, you can take that same authority
and silence the rising emotional storm inside you.
Tell yourself, "Peace, be still."

This person is full of pride and understands nothing,
but is sick with a love for arguing and fighting about words.
This brings jealousy, fighting, speaking against others, evil mistrust.

1 Timothy 6:4 ncv

December 4

Always keep pressing on
knowing I'm with you.
When you admit your human weakness,
and rise up out of the swamp of fear,
you won't be bitten by pride and envy.
Don't allow your faith
to come to a stand-still
by neglecting our time together.
Faith that becomes stagnant goes nowhere,
like standing water that grows mold
and attracts the snakes of discontent.
Don't allow yourself
to be yanked from the sweetness
of our beautiful communication.
I'm here to give you everything.
When you're weak, I'm strong in you.
I want to give you abilities
you didn't know possible.

I cried to God in my distress and he answered me.
He freed me from all my fears!

PSALM 34:4 TPT

December 5

Other people's problems
don't define who you are.
Another's problems
don't reflect your character.
Remove from your life
everything that's untrustworthy
and unclean.
Concentrate on that which is good,
true, honest, and pure
and you'll attract these attributes in others.
You can't mend the devil's ways.
Don't even try.
When My children are betrayed or lied to,
I see all. Nothing escapes My eye.
Recompense is Mine.
Put everything in My hands.

Do not take revenge, my dear friends, but leave room for God's wrath,
for it is written: "It is mine to avenge; I will repay," says the Lord.

ROMANS 12:19 NIV

December 6

When I walked the earth,
I walked with humility
to show you how to walk with
the radiance of simplicity.
Today, welcome the rich rewards
in honoring the path
of humility. The wealthy soul prospers
without the grief of self-promotion
or efforts for personal gain.
My desire is
for you to know
the profound experience
of love without walls.

"Remember this: If you have a lofty opinion of yourself and seek to
be honored, you will be humbled. But if you have a modest opinion of
yourself and choose to humble yourself, you will be honored."

MATTHEW 23:12 TPT

December 7

When you try to run things on your own,
let Me ask you if you'd mind
helping Me with the matter of the sunrise.
All you have to do is pull up the golden hues of dawn
against the din of night and tell the stars
to take a rest. You see, I'm making roads through
desert lands and rivers across a cold, hard earth,
and I'd like your expert assistance.
I was wondering if you'd be so good as to create
a crocodile for Me or maybe a rose out of nothing.
Say, maybe you could put together an entire galaxy!
I love you dearly, but why fire Me as God
and take over the world and your life all by yourself?
Be patient a little while longer, dear one,
everything is going to work out perfectly
if you'll just let Me be God.

Have you commanded the morning since your days began,
and caused the dawn to know its place,
that it might take hold of the skirts of the earth,
and the wicked be shaken out of it?

JOB 38:12-13 ESV

December 8

You now stand upon the threshold of new beginnings.
Old "things" are quickly passing away from you,
and you can expect all "things" to become new.
You can expect what's been so important
to you yesterday to begin to lose
its luster. This is because I'm calling you
to a higher place and a deeper relationship
with Me. The joys you'll experience with Me
far outweigh all temporary pleasures you've experienced
without Me. I want to be at the helm of your life.
I want to be your all-in-all. I want you to
trust and hold onto the daily promises I give you.
As you worship Me, I'll renew your mind
and cleanse all leftover fragments of wasted time.
I'm restoring everything
and making all things new for you.

Do not be conformed to this world, but be transformed by the
renewing of your mind, so that you may prove what the will of God is,
that which is good and acceptable and perfect.

ROMANS 12:2 NASB

December 9

I love your laughter, and I want you to know
I'm in your tears, as well. Not one
tear falls that I don't catch.
I love the sweet worship
you lift up to Me from your pure
and renewed heart and mind.
Today, remember that you're
a treasure to Me.
Tell yourself that you're a treasure
to Me when you sit down and when
you stand up. Feel My love for you
as you carry on throughout this day.
You may forget Me, but I never forget you.
Your precious face is always before Me.

Those who sow their tears as seeds
will reap a harvest with joyful shouts of glee.

PSALM 126:5 TPT

December 10

Some people believe they're just fine
in My eyes because they've given
their assent to the idea that I exist.
I don't respond to the mere assent that
I exist. Human philosophies may be fascinating,
but they don't forgive sin and transform the heart.
I'm the giver of life.
I'm not a distant relative to connect with on holidays.
Nice thoughts and good wishes aren't prayers.
I came to impart, provide, and multiply My power
in the world through My own. Everything I give you
is good, and I empower you to live beyond
your own resources. Believe what I'm telling you,
and you'll see miracles abound in your life.
Keep your heart far from the foolishness
of man's devices today.
You're much bigger than you think.

"Now you understand that I have imparted to you all my authority to
trample over his kingdom. You will trample upon every demon before
you and overcome every power Satan possesses. Absolutely nothing
will be able to harm you as you walk in this authority."

LUKE 10:19 TPT

December 11

I know this is a busy time and
I'm opening a new pattern of thinking
to you, one filled with joy and the expectation
of good things. The devil has tried to grip you
with habits of negative thinking and behavior.
It's time to put an end to these.
The power of My Spirit is alive in you,
and you're much smarter than you think.
The work that I'm doing in your life
is momentous. I'm revealing more of Myself
and My mind to you every day. Don't allow
yourself to be distracted because I have so much
to show you and teach you. Come closer
and receive everything you need to fulfill
all your plans.

Don't let anyone capture you with empty philosophies and high-
sounding nonsense that come from human thinking and from the
spiritual powers of this world, rather than from Christ.

COLOSSIANS 2:8 NLT

December 12

Be released right now
from the influence of the world
and your old tendency to be stressed and vulnerable.
Those days are gone!
I want our minds to be united as one mind.
I've told you to delight yourself in Me,
and you'll know more of heavenly delight
as your life and Mine create one life,
and your heart beats fervently against Mine.
You'll see miracles on a daily basis as you
draw closer to Me in all your ways.
I want our relationship to be unique,
wondrous, and joyous.

He has taught you to let go of the lifestyle of the ancient man, the old
self - life, which was corrupted by sinful and deceitful desires that spring
from delusions. Now it's time to be made new by every revelation
that's been given to you.

EPHESIANS 4:22-23 TPT

December 13

When you think about
My giving and taking away,
think as I think.
I give blessings, and I take away curses.
I give happiness and joy, and I take away depression.
I give peace, and I take away fear.
I give hope, and I take away despair.
I give life, and I take away futility.
I give the oil of joy, and I take away the spirit of heaviness.
I give provision and plenty, and I take away poverty and
lack.
I give you heaven, and I take away the agony of hell.
I want you to know more of My nature
and who I am because then you'll begin
to live even more fully in the overcoming
power-infused life I've given you.

Blessed be the God and Father of our Lord Jesus Christ, who has
blessed us with every spiritual blessing in the heavenly places in Christ.

EPHESIANS 1:3 NKJV

December 14

I don't make bad things happen
to teach you a lesson.
That's not like Me at all!
It's My nature to give good.
It's written, "Every good and perfect gift
comes from above, from the Father of Lights,"
that's every good and perfect gift,
dear one, not leaving anything out
that's good because your heavenly Father
is good. The Father and I are one,
and you can expect good things
to come your way because you'll
learn long-lasting lessons through
goodness that'll blaze the trail for more
goodness. Think about all the good
things you receive from Me every day!
Concentrate on what is good and you'll
be a carrier of goodness wherever you go,
attracting even more good!

The LORD is good and does what is right;
he shows the proper path to those who go astray.

PSALM 25:8 NLT

December 15

I give you free choice, not only in your actions,
but in the way you think. When you want something
that'll eventually bite you on the toe,
I won't stop you, but know that your choices
have consequences. I want you to choose
My ways, not yours. I want you to attract
blessings and goodness to yourself.
Today, choose to think beautiful thoughts.
Choose to act justly with integrity.
Those who choose evil will reap evil,
but not you! You, dear child, will always
reap goodness and blessings as you stick
close to Me, making powerful spirit-filled
choices. Today, you'll have opportunities
to choose which way to go. Choose Me.

If serving the LORD seems undesirable to you, then choose for
yourselves this day whom you will serve, whether the gods your
ancestors served beyond the Euphrates, or the gods of the Amorites,
in whose land you are living. But as for me and my household, we will
serve the LORD.

JOSHUA 24:15 NIV

December 16

Everything is perfect in My timing.
There are no missing fragments or holes
in time when you're Mine.
There are no second-hand promises
in My kingdom, no expired guarantees.
There's no down-sizing in heaven's economy,
no lay-offs or walking papers;
there's never a lull in activity, and
never is a single moment lost.
Time can't stray from Me, can't disappear
or drop off-course into the abyss.
Think of yourself in terms of the immortal clock,
one that never reads "Too Late."
Not a single hour passes unheralded by Me.
I am God and I possess all time.
I control all, and I've put you on earth
for such a time as this. You're right on
target, dear one, you're right on time.

"I listened to you at the time of my favor. And the day when you needed salvation, I came to your aid." So can't you see? Now is the time to respond to his favor! Now is the day of salvation!

2 CORINTHIANS 6:2 TPT

December 17

I'm the Lord who heals you
and makes you whole.
I'm the Lord who lifts you up
above yourself.
I'm the Lord who gives
you all things good.
I'm a giving God and I love you.
Be hugged and loved by Me today.

"I love each of you with the same love that the Father loves me.
You must continually let my love nourish your hearts.
If you keep my commands, you will live in my love,
just as I have kept my Father's commands,
for I continually live nourished and empowered by his love."

JOHN 15:9-10 TPT

December 18

See yourself today as I see you.
You're Mine and I'm yours.
I'm answering the prayers of your heart today.
I don't withhold My goodness,
nor will I ever withhold My goodness
from you. I'm a giving God and I love you!
Today, let Me refresh you. Let Me invigorate
and energize you. I'm the God of all there is and
I'm yours. See yourself as renewed and restored
in Me. See yourself empowered. You're precious
in the world you've been called to
at this time, so I may live in you and through you.
My Holy Spirit will touch the world
through your hands and feet and mind
and heart. You're uniquely designed and
created to be who you are.
Be confident today; be glad today.
Be filled with expectation, for I have much to show you,
and you have much to give.

We have become his poetry, a re-created people that will fulfill the
destiny he has given each of us, for we are joined to Jesus,
the Anointed One.

EPHESIANS 2:10 TPT

December 19

Today is the day you'll see
the sun shining on problems
you thought would never be solved.
Today is the day to take a look
into your heart and see
that which you've worried
about needlessly. Observe and be aware,
lest you worry needlessly tomorrow,
for worry doesn't stir the heart of heaven.
It's faith that stirs the heart of heaven.
Faith brings the realization of everything
you hope for and dream of,
everything you want and desire.

**Trust in the LORD and do good;
dwell in the land and cultivate faithfulness.**

PSALM 37:3 NASB

December 20

Live this day as a journey.
I'm walking beside you and within you.
Your feet are My feet.
Your eyes are My eyes.
Your ears are My ears.
I'll bring out in you every lovely
and wonderful thing that'll help you
know yourself better. In knowing
who you are in Me, you'll be
more open to those around you.
I know your desires,
and I want you to know
that the desires of your heart
are birthed in Mine.

"You shall follow the LORD your God and fear Him;
and you shall keep His commandments,
listen to His voice, serve Him, and cling to Him."

DEUTERONOMY 13:4 NASB

December 21

Think of Me as your dearest companion,
for no one knows you as I know you.
No one knows your heart
as I know your heart.
Allow Me to be
your source of joy today
because I want you to take some time
to have fun, to laugh,
and to allow yourself to rest
and be happy.

You prepare a meal for me in front of my enemies.
You pour oil of blessing on my head;
you fill my cup to overflowing.

PSALM 23:5 NKJV

December 22

Don't be afraid of loneliness.
When the long, hard hand
of loneliness reaches for you,
don't be so swift to escape
its touch. Loneliness can season
you like a spice,
can you show you things
about yourself you didn't know.
Allow loneliness to speak to your soul
so you hear My voice and understand
your absolute need for Me.
When you rest awhile with loneliness,
you'll raise your head higher
when it lifts and realize
you're never alone with Me.
Come and keep Me company.

Whoever dwells in the shelter of the Most High
will rest in the shadow of the Almighty. I will say of the LORD,
"He is my refuge and my fortress, my God, in whom I trust."

PSALM 91:1-2 NIV

December 23

The less strength you think you have,
the more I can pour My strength
into you. My strength
is made perfect in weakness.
I can, and in your natural strength,
you can't.
I pour Myself into you by My Spirit
and then wonderfully,
My Spirit flows out through you
and the world is touched
and changed. Set your agenda aside today.
Trust Me to work through you because
the work you do is Mine, not yours.
Be courageous and give
every hint of weakness to Me.
Feel your courage
increase in you today.

"Not by might nor by power,
but by My Spirit," says the Lord.

ZECHARIAH 4:6 NKJV

December 24

You're going to see Me move
in a new and intriguing way on this,
the day that's celebrated as the eve of My birth.
Observe carefully, for I often move suddenly,
but you'll know as you pause to listen,
as you still your mind,
and when you open your eyes to see.
You've been called and honored by Me.
I honor you because you honor and
trust Me as the source
of all you are and have.
You hear Me and know My voice.

"Whoever serves me must follow me.
Then my servant will be with me everywhere I am.
My Father will honor anyone who serves me."

JOHN 12:26 NCV

December 25

Today, on the day My birth is celebrated,
I heal you.
I'm healing everything that has caused
you pain, discomfort, and unhappiness.
I heal you.
I restore your hope and pour out
My blessing on your tender heart.
I came to save you and free you
from the cares and ills of the world,
so today on My birthday, let your faith
bubble up as happiness
and goodness flow through you.
Praise Me in song and in expressions of joy.
Draw close to Me and walk
in your healing with both hands in Mine,
refreshed, whole, and new.
My love has made you complete.

"I will bring health and healing to it;
I will heal my people and will let them
enjoy abundant peace and security."

JEREMIAH 33:6 NIV

December 26

There's nothing that can separate us.
Nothing can take you from Me
except yourself. No devil has the power
to take you from My tender grip.
Only you have the power
to turn your face from Me,
and that is why I love it when your face
is pressed against Mine,
and we walk together in this journey
of life that I've given you.
You'll live out your years with the glory
of God before you, around you, behind you,
and in you. I haven't called you to walk
a tough road, one with filled with broken glass
and rubble. No, I have called you to walk
with My arms around you, holding you,
and talking to you continually.
Every moment you breathe,
My breath breathes in yours.

Then the LORD God formed man of dust from the ground,
and breathed into his nostrils the breath of life;
and man became a living being.

GENESIS 2:7 NASB

December 27

You're called to reign
and to carry yourself as a child of the King.
I've removed feelings of inferiority
and shame off the throne of your life.
Today, you're sitting in a position of royalty.
As My child, and a beneficiary
of all that I have,
handle yourself from now on
with royal confidence,
knowing that the God of all creation
walks beside you,
and you're wearing
your crown of blessing.

Since we are his true children, we qualify to share all his treasures,
for indeed, we are heirs of God himself. And since we are joined
to Christ, we also inherit all that he is and all that he has. We will
experience being co-glorified with him provided that we accept his
sufferings as our own.

ROMANS 8:17 TPT

December 28

You travel today along a highway
crowded with others going in the same direction,
and many travel with different intent.
There'll be stop-and-go moments for you,
moments when you feel as though
you'll be stuck in the traffic jam of life forever.
You'll look to the left and to the right,
and you'll see others speeding along
ahead of you. Take a look at the drivers,
dear one. Who's in the driver's seat?
You're Mine and I'm yours,
and I'm in the driver's seat of your vehicle.
If you think you're stalled on the highway
of today's journey, know that when
I'm at the wheel, you're never stalled.
Nothing–no, nothing–can stop or delay you.
I'm not a God of delays. Be at peace,
in Me; everything is right on time.

**"I continually see the Lord in front of me.
He's at my right hand, and I am never shaken."**

ACTS 2:25 TPT

December 29

I walk with you today
in every step you take.
I'm with you as you eat your meals,
and as you prepare your day.
I'm with you as you do your work.
I am with you as you dress yourself.
Nothing separates us in the hours
that you live this day.
As you sleep, I kiss your closed eyelids.
I caress you in your sleep,
and remind you in your dreams
that you are My chosen, My beloved one.

"Yes, many are invited,
but only a few are chosen."

MATTHEW 22:14 NCV

December 30

If you believe the miles ahead
look too difficult,
and you have too far to go,
I'm telling you the miles ahead
for you are wonderful and full of adventure.
I'm giving you a life of discovery.
Take the new. Take the fresh. Take the unknown.
Don't be afraid to take the road less traveled.
Don't be afraid of change.
Take the high road today.
Set aside your worldly concerns
and join the chorus of angels that praise Me.
Give thanks for the life I've given you
and love the journey.

**It is God who arms me with strength
and keeps my way secure.**

Psalm 18:32 niv

December 31

You're standing on the threshold of a new year,
and I have great things in store for you.
At the close of these last twelve months,
be glad for what you've seen
and accomplished in your life.
Be glad for your spiritual growth
and My blessing on you.
Glimpses of My glory have been seen through
much suffering and turmoil
in the world, and now I'm preparing
to send a downpour of My Holy Spirit to the earth
as I've promised in My Word.
Many shall come to experience
the reality of who I am
and the glory of My power
in an unprecedented awakening.
Get ready.

"I will pour out my Spirit upon all people.
Your sons and daughters will prophesy.
Your old men will dream dreams,
and your young men will see visions."

JOEL 2:28-29 NLT